Developing a Creative and Innovative Integrated Marketing Communications Plan: A Working Model

James R. Ogden
Kutztown University of Pennsylvania

Prentice Hall, Upper Saddle River, New Jersey 07458

Acquisitions Editor: Gabrielle Dudnyk
Associate Editor: John Larkin
Editorial Assistant: Michele Foresta
Editor-in-Chief: Jim Boyd
Marketing Manager: Shannon Moore
Production Editor Liaison: Michelle Rich
Managing Editor: Dee Josephson
Associate Managing Editor: Linda DeLorenzo
Manufacturing Buyer: Diane Peirano
Manufacturing Supervisor: Arnold Vila
Manufacturing Manager: Vincent Scelta
Cover Director: Jayne Conte
Cover Design: Karen Salzbach
Illustrator (Interior): BookMasters, Inc.
Composition: BookMasters, Inc.

Library of Congress Cataloging-in-Publication Data

Ogden, James R.
    Developing a creative and innovative integrated marketing
communications plan : a working model / James R. Ogden.
        p.   cm.
    ISBN 0–13–778333–7
    1. Communication in marketing.   I. Title
HF5415.123.037   1998
658.8'02—dc21   98-4437
                                                 CIP

Prentice-Hall International (UK) Limited, London
Prentice-Hall of Australia Pty. Limited, Sydney
Prentice-Hall Canada, Inc., Toronto
Prentice-Hall Hispanoamericana, S.A., Mexico
Prentice-Hall of India Private Limited, New Delhi
Prentice-Hall of Japan, Inc., Tokyo
Simon & Schuster Asia Pte Ltd., Singapore
Editora Prentice-Hall do Brasil, Ltda., Rio de Janeiro

Printed in the United States of America

10 9 8 7 6 5 4 3 2 1

Contents

Introduction:
The Development of an Integrated Marketing Communication Plan—A Working Model

Imagine you're planning a trip from New York City to Aspen, Colorado. You must be in Aspen in four days from your date of departure. Your finances are tight, so flying is out of the question. Your only option is to drive. You've always wanted to see the countryside anyway, so you plan your highway journey. You invest in some maps to chart your course.

What questions must you answer as you plan your trip? First you need to reach Aspen within four days. Can you drive that far in the allotted amount of time? How much time do you allow for unexpected delays, like bad weather or car trouble? How much time do you allow for sightseeing? Second, you don't have that much money—after all, if you did you'd be flying—so what's your budget for meals, motels, and gasoline?

Building an integrated marketing communication (IMC) plan is like planning your cross-country trip. The IMC plan is your marketing road map. It helps you to conceive a concrete plan of action. You develop a starting point and a destination. How do you reach that destination from where you're starting? What's your timetable? What's your budget?

No perfect plan exists that will fit every IMC planner's needs or wants. The following plan was created to give the IMC planner an outline that is flexible yet simple and clear. This outline should be used like a template, or a guide. Feel free to insert or delete as the individual case requires. If sections or ideas do not fit your needs, simply omit them from the overall plan. Sequencing is important in IMC planning. In some cases, the sequence of this model can be changed to meet the needs of the planner. The information in this book does include ALL essential elements necessary to create an effective IMC plan. Throughout the book, space has been left for the reader to jot down thoughts and fill in areas that will be needed for the overall plan development. Additionally, sources of information have been included to help you, as an IMC planner, secure data and information necessary for a comprehensive and workable plan. Appendices have been included to allow easy access to information that will assist in IMC planning.

This book was written to assist those involved in IMC planning. Because of the perforated pages, which make the book easy to use, I would suggest investing in three 3-ring binders. The first can be used to insert pages from the book that contain resource information, such as the appendices. You can also include information and data from outside sources, thus expanding your database. Until you've "memorized" the flowcharts, I would recommend tearing them out and attaching them to the front and back covers of the binders to allow easy reference.

Use the second binder to help build your personal IMC plan. Throughout the book, templates allow for easy fill-in the blanks. As you go through the book, simply fill in the blanks, tear them out, and place them in the second binder. When you've finished reading the book, you'll have a completed, comprehensive IMC plan.

For the college student, the third binder can be used for text pages that serve as notes. Each of the sections will follow information that your professor is providing. Simply tear out the pages that you are currently discussing, take them to class, and then insert them in the third binder.

After you've finished reading the book, you'll have a three-ring library of information and data about integrated marketing communication and a personal IMC plan.

WHAT IS INTEGRATED MARKETING COMMUNICATONS?

Picture yourself in the supermarket, looking for a particular brand of beans. As you scan the shelves, you see many labels. What makes you choose a particular brand from among the many competitors? Is it the packaging? Perhaps the actual brand name? Is it the brand's position on the shelf? Maybe you've read about the product in the newspaper? Perhaps you've seen the product on television? Could it be that a friend told you how much he liked the product? Or maybe your friend didn't like one or two of the other brands. Does the supermarket even have the brand that you're looking for? Do you have a coupon you can use? Does the price appeal to you as a price-conscious consumer? The answer may be that any one or all of the above caused you to select that can of beans. Of course, there may have been many other variables that played a part in your decision. In the end, it's the overall perception you have toward the product that leads you to your purchase decision.

It is necessary for businesses and marketers, in today's competitive market, to make sure that the messages consumers receive about products or services are *clear, concise,* and *integrated.* In other words, every member of the corporation or organization involved in the marketing of a product or service must be giving the consumer the same message.

Put yourself back in the supermarket, trying to make the best choice of the cans of beans offered for sale. Do you as a consumer think about all of the elements involved in the production of the beans, from processing to human resources? From the law department to the transportation department? Of course you don't. You don't look at that can of beans and say, "Wow, look at what those accountants did!" or "Gosh, those corporate trainers really messed up this time." When consumers look at a product or service, they're only looking for those qualities that will satisfy a need or a want that they brought with them into the store. All those messages they've received about the product or service from television, radio, friends, family, and so on become important to the purchase decision. Because of this, businesspeople need to make sure that the messages they are sending to their targeted consumers are accurate, concise, and consistent. The message being sent to the consumer must be an integrated communication.

When consumers receive different messages, or worse yet, messages that conflict, they have a hard time picking out which things to believe. Have you ever had a friend recommend a can of beans, telling you that they're the best tasting beans she's ever eaten? Then you buy the beans and eat them, and you are disappointed because there's nothing unique about them. The same thing can happen in consumer communication. The public relations (PR) department may be sending a message about how a new "wonder" product can clean anything, while the advertising people are placing ads on television, telling the consumer to use this new product only on plastic laminated counters. It's a mixed message that not only costs the business and consumer time and money but also confuses the consumer. It is therefore necessary to integrate all consumer communications so that everyone is providing the same message.

Businesses must recognize that all their marketing and communication variables affect one another, the consumer, and the communicators. It follows, then, that all communication variables will have an effect on marketing. Because of this, all communications from an organization must be integrated. The outcome of integration is the creation of *synergy*. The concept of synergy, as used in business situations, is that the combined efforts of all business units result in a greater effect than those of individual or unit efforts.

This book gives a model that creates an integrated and synergistic IMC plan.

CHAPTER

Marketing and IMC

1

THE MARKETING CONCEPT

Simply stated, the marketing concept says that a company should satisfy consumer wants and needs at a profit. In other words, the company or organization should aim all of its efforts toward giving its customers the services and products that they want or need. By doing so, the business creates happy customers, which translates to increased sales and profits. Why is it so hard to grasp this concept? Doesn't it sound easy? The problem with the integration of the marketing concept into today's businesses and organizations is that many top executives learned different methods of management. The old adage, "You can't teach an old dog new tricks," may be one of the stumbling blocks to the adoption of a customer orientation.

Remember that the production process became popular when Henry Ford began to market the Model T. One of the quotations attributed to Mr. Ford was that the customer could have any color of car he wanted as long as it was black. Mr. Ford, in other words, had a *production orientation*. Many businesses are organized around departments, which are set up to specialize in given tasks. For example, the accounting department "accounts" for all funds. The production department is concerned only with getting the product manufactured. The finance department only cares about the company's cash position and liquidity. Finally, the sales department is concerned only with soliciting orders from the customers. If the company makes money, everyone is happy. If not, there are significant number of "career readjustments" for the employees. With this system, companies and organizations build fences around their duties. They became territorial in nature and want no part of corporate overlapping. Each territory needs to be protected by the departmental managers, who may fear for their jobs. Because of these organizational structures, it has been hard to sell the marketing concept to many businesses and organizations, but without it there are decreased sales and profits.

Recently, more and more firms have embraced the marketing concept and have undertaken the process of reengineering or restructuring their organizations. Others still operate with the production orientation. Clearly, the marketing concept is logical, but for many organizations very hard to adopt.

The marketing concept should be taken a step further in relation to customer satisfaction. It helps an organization to rethink the definition of the marketing concept and to expand it by replacing the words "satisfy customer needs" with "exceed customer expectations." It is far better to exceed the expectations of the consumer than to just meet them. Two companies that have recently embraced this idea are Boston Market and Wal-Mart: Each set up a different level of expectation and then gave the consumers more than they expected.

Wal-Mart, for example, told the consumer it was a discount store but offered more than the traditional discounter. Not only did it have low prices, but it had clean rest rooms, liberal return policies, and a slightly higher level of service than its competitors.

Boston Market provides fast food. Yet, in the fast-food category, it has developed a product that is perceived as wholesome and better tasting than its competitors. The customer expects typical fast food but receives a product far above expectations. Boston Market has created a new category in food marketing called "designer fast food."

Because, in marketing, customer perception is reality, people involved in communication management must be sure to create the correct expectations for the customer and then try to exceed them. This task is not easy. Every member of the organization has to be involved in this IMC process and to understand what is being communicated to the customer. The advertising people cannot advise the consumer to "fly the friendly skies," only to have that person treated in a less than friendly fashion. The company has to be sure that the service or product delivers what was promised. By embracing the marketing concept, this task becomes easier.

THE RELATIONSHIP BETWEEN MARKETING AND IMC

Integrated marketing communications is an expansion of the promotion element of the marketing mix. It is essentially the recognition of the importance of communicating the same message to the targeted markets. In addition, it is the recognition that all of the IMC variables communicate and that there is an overlap in the communication these variables provide. Each of the IMC variables affects the overall marketing program, so they all must be managed to exploit their effectiveness.

To have effective integration in the communications area, it is necessary to understand the marketing functions. Figure 1–1, *Doc Ogden's Marketing Flowchart,* is an outline of the marketing management process utilized by many companies.

The marketing management process is a clearly defined and orderly flow of steps, taken to ensure that all of the marketing functions are performed and integrated to provide the highest-quality, most effective marketing plan possible. Each of the phases of the marketing management plan rely on the various other phases for information and guidance. The plan includes the following steps.

Company or Organizational Mission and/or Vision

The **mission statement** is simply the reason that the company or organization exists. It may include a series of goals or objectives that the organization wishes to achieve or strive for. It usually refers to giving a financial return to the stakeholders of the company or organization. For example, suppose you want to be the world's largest children's apparel retailer. In this case your mission may read "to be the world's largest retailer of children's apparel, while providing a significant return to our shareholders."

> The mission describes the present condition of the company; it defines the business, and it defines the industry.

The **vision statement** is closely related to the mission statement, but it looks to the future. Where does the organization or company see itself in the future? What does the company expect to be doing? The vision statement should be developed with input from all of the company's (or organization's) stakeholders. The stakeholders include the management, employees, stockholders, consumers, and public.

> The vision defines the plans for the future shared by all members
> of the organization; it defines who the company is, what it does,
> and most important, where it's headed.

Situation Analysis

The **situation analysis** is basically just a history of the company. Where is the company now and how did it get there? It should include, among other things, the company's growth, history, product offerings, sales volume, and markets. Also included is an analysis of the various environments that may have an impact on the organization. These may include (but aren't limited to) social, economic, technological, legal, political, competitive and natural environments. To fully understand these environments, the marketing department, in conjunction with the various other corporate departments, undertakes a process known as environmental scanning. With environmental scanning the company can identify those environments that may have an impact on the firm, as well as predict the occurrence of these changes and their relevant force. The marketing manager

FIGURE 1–1 Doc Ogden's Marketing Management Flowchart

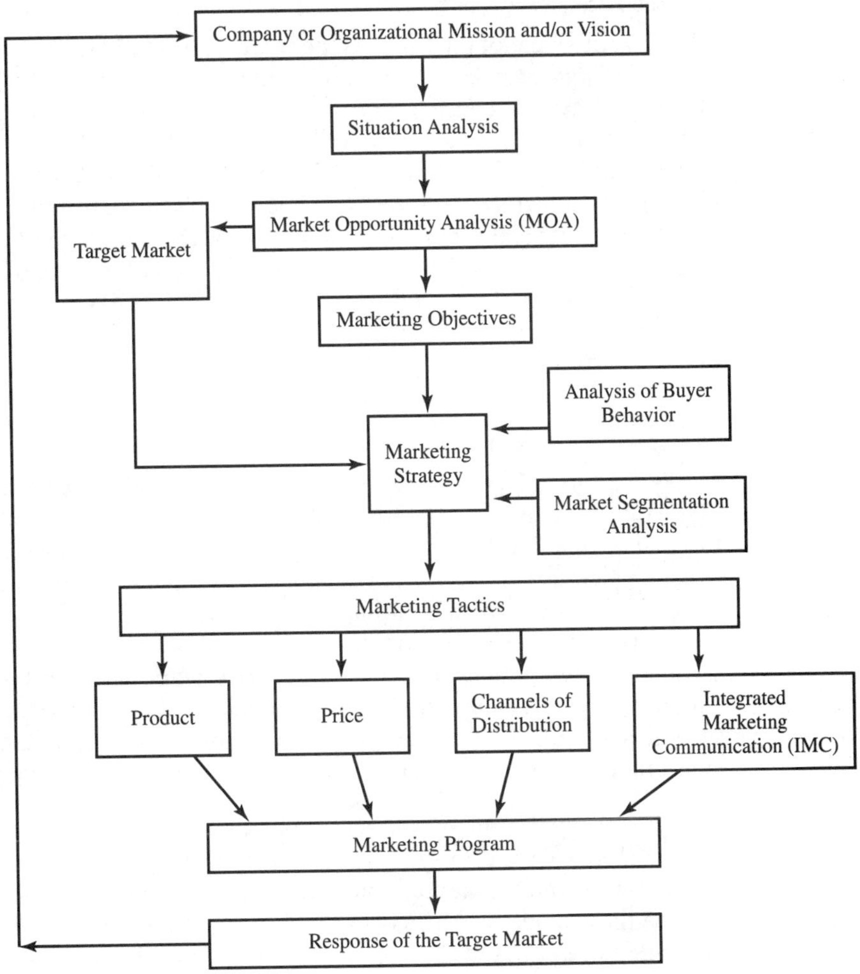

continually looks to the corporate mission to identify those environments that could affect the company. With this information, the organization can develop responses to environmental changes. In this way the company is being *proactive* rather than *reactive*. Thus the marketers can concentrate on the next step of the marketing management process, which is market opportunity analysis.

Market Opportunity Analysis

Market opportunity analysis (MOA) is simply the process of trying to discover which markets offer the best opportunity for exploitation by the company or organization. Numerous tools, both qualitative and quantitative, are used to help identify the markets and assess their relative importance. For example, the marketers may wish to develop a quantitative forecasting formula to help assess the overall sales volume for a particular market. Numerous statistical techniques can be used, casual modeling being among the most popular. Similarly, qualitative techniques can be used to assess consumer perceptions. One of the more popular is the focus group, which can reveal consumers' biases and perceptions about a given product or service. Overall, the idea behind an MOA is to aid the marketer in discovering which markets would be effective targets for the company's products and services.

Target Market

A natural outcome of the MOA is the **target market (TM),** the group of people toward whom the organization or company decides to aim its marketing efforts. This group is defined by a typical-consumer profile, and included are only people who (1) are willing to buy the product, (2) are able to buy the product (both physically and monetarily), and (3) are the final consumers in the market. It is a mistake to count the number of products manufactured or forecasted because this number is likely to be too high or too low. An ongoing count of users is essential for the overall marketing plan to be effective. Armed with a TM, the marketer can then look at the overall market and decide if it should be broken down into smaller groups, a process known as market segmentation. In addition, the TM is redefined and placed in the company's or organization's marketing strategy (which will be discussed later).

Marketing Objectives

Marketing objectives are goals the organization feels it wants, or needs, to achieve. These objectives are specific to the marketing department and specific time guidelines for goal completion. The marketing objectives are simply logical deductions from the situation analysis and MOA. For example, if one marketer forecasted sales of $400,000, a logical objective would be to increase sales to $400,000. Objectives are goals for the future, as well as a predication of future trends (a forecast). Objectives may deal with satisfying of the public, unit sales targets, overall dollar sales targets, channels of distribution targets, or any number of marketing-related goals. All objectives should be specific and realistic. They can be either quantitative or qualitative, but they must be measurable, to let the marketers know if they have been achieved.

Marketing Strategy

Given the overall marketing objectives, the marketer's next step is to decide how to achieve these objectives. The plan that is used to accomplish this task is known as the **marketing strategy.** A marketing strategy is the "big picture," the total directional thrust of the marketing to be employed. It should include a description of the targeted markets, as well as a strategic decision for each one. Also included should be segmentation decisions and consumer behavior analysis and decisions. A strategy may include product differentiation techniques, price and quality, and positioning. It should be used as a guide for the development of the executionable tactics (which will be discussed later).

Analysis of Buyer Behavior

Marketers need and want information about the consumers that are purchasing the company's products (or that may purchase the products given the right marketing). Data on **buyer or consumer behavior** may include demographics, geographics, or psychographics (life-style analysis). By learning how and why people purchase their products, the marketers can tailor their marketing tactics to these audiences. For example, Al Hirt may be a good spokesperson for New Orleans jazz. He may not be a good spokesperson, however, for New Age music. The whole idea behind the analysis of consumer behavior is to find information to help describe and predict what the company's consumers will do now and in the future.

Market Segmentation Analysis

There may be situations in which the marketers don't want to or can't pursue an entire target market to exploit it for profits. One step in determining the type or style of marketing that will be undertaken is **market segmentation analysis.** The idea is to look for consumer *response behavior.* In other words, the marketer wants to know what makes an individual respond to a given cue in the environment. Each group of consumers that responds in the same way is placed in a subgroup, or market segment. These subgroups should be homogeneous within the major group (in other words, all members of one group should respond in the same way) but as heterogeneous (or different) as possible between groups. In other words, within any one group, the consumers are motivated to act or buy in the same way, but between each of the different groups there should be a big difference in the way they respond to marketing. If segmentation is needed, a separate strategy and tactical executions are used to reach that subgroup. If segmentation is not required, the company can use a mass marketing approach to reach its targeted market. Either way, the information obtained from the market segmentation analysis is used to facilitate accurate strategy development.

Marketing Tactics

Marketing tactics are the executable elements of the marketing plan. They are the actual steps undertaken by marketers. Included are four elements of marketing known as the *marketing mix:* product, price, channels of distribution, and integrated marketing communications. For each of these tactical areas, specific actions are spelled out for employees and marketers in terms of who should undertake what function and when. The marketing manager must be sure that there is integration among each of the mix variables. This helps to create a marketing synergy for the company and also helps to detect weaknesses in the marketing executions. For a better understanding of the relationship of the marketing mix variables, a short discussion of the marketing program is needed.

Marketing Program

The **marketing program** is simply all the plans from the marketing mix, integrated and placed in order of execution, as well as resource allocation. The marketing manager must decide how much money is to be given to each of the various elements of the marketing mix and how much should be allocated *within* each of the mix variables. Besides capital allocation, the marketing program includes information about human resource allocation: who gets whom, when, why, and where.

Product

The **product** mix includes information about how a product is developed and the plan that is being used to bring it to market. Included is the "total product concept," that is, the idea that a given product or service is much more than just the physical good or service. The product is made up of (1) consumer or user benefits, (2) want- or need-satisfying attributes, (3) physical goods or services, (4) packaging, (5) branding, and (6) labeling. Without each of these areas, companies and organizations would not be able to differentiate their products or services from those of the competition. In addition, the marketers must develop objectives and strategies for executing product development and management.

Price

Decisions must be made about a product's price. Just as in all the other product decisions, the price variable also needs objectives and strategies for development. Each decision about the price variable must be integrated and have synergy with the other mix variables. For example, the promotion people should not develop promotions that show what a great buy a product is if the pricing strategy is to develop high-quality imaging by charging a high price. In addition to objectives, price decision makers need to take into account the flexibility of price (called price elasticity) by looking at buyers, costs, and competition. Price policies are created to give the pricing manager a "track" to run on for the decision-making process. The last step in pricing is to actually set, or establish, prices for the various products or services. These steps are undertaken whether the organization is profit-based or non-profit, and whether it produces a service or a product.

Channels of Distribution

Channels of distribution are used to get the product from the manufacturer, or service provider, to the final consumer. Again, as in product and price, the channels of distribution managers are concerned with the development of objectives and strategies needed to successfully reach the consumer. The overall process of developing a channel of distribution is called a *physical distribution system* (PDS). The overall management of the process is referred to as *physical distribution management* (PDM). In developing a PDS the manager is concerned with strategy and its integration into the overall marketing program. In addition, numerous decisions are made about the type of channel system desired, its design, and its overall management. Channel objectives should reflect performance, the extent of control over the channel, and the financial support available to build and manage it. In addition, the physical distribution manager is concerned with facilities (manufacturing plants, warehouses, retail outlets, etc.): quantity, size, location, capital outlay, and operating costs. Another concern is inventory: economic order, just-in-time capability, speed of delivery, levels of stock, and so on. Handling and storage, communications, and transportation are also areas of concern for those involved in the management of the physical distribution system. It is imperative that the systems themselves, as well as their management, be synergetic and integrated with other marketing areas.

Integrated Marketing Communication

The **integrated marketing communication (IMC)** mix is made up of a number of mixed variables, including (1) public relations and publicity, (2) direct marketing, (3) advertising, (4) personal selling, (5) cybermarketing, and (6) sales promotion. Much more information about these areas will be given later. It is enough to say here that they must all be integrated and must be communicating the same thing to all stakeholders and consumers.

Evaluation and Control

In every organization or business, there is a need for regular monitoring of the performance of all marketing activities. The steps taken to ensure that the marketing plan is in line with the corporate mission and marketing objectives are called **evaluation and control.** Although much of the previous discussion has centered around the development of a marketing plan, in reality most of the marketer's time is spent on evaluating and controlling the marketing activities. Planning is very important during the early stages of marketing; however, once the project is off the ground, the main emphasis is on control. Numerous activities are developed to help the marketing manager in the evaluation and control process. For example, formal tools, such as focus groups, feedback sheets, and quantifiable statistics (sales figures, audience reach, etc.) can help the marketing manager evaluate the effectiveness of a campaign.

Many actions are undertaken to allow the marketing manager to identify performance gaps in the overall marketing program. In addition, changes may be needed in tactical executions or strategies. Remember, the *only constant in the universe is change.* Because change occurs in the marketing environment, change must also occur in the overall marketing plan. Generally, to allow for evaluation and control, standards of measurement are specified so that performance can be monitored. If problems can be foreseen (or forecasted), proactive strategies can be developed. Because of the costs associated with the development of a marketing plan, evaluation and control are essential elements and should occur at every decision-making step.

Response of the Target Market

The final step in the marketing plan is a form of evaluation and control. To see if all elements of the marketing plan are working and on target, the **response of the target market** must be monitored. In general, the response of the target market is measured by evaluating such statistics as market share, sales in units, profitability, audience reach, and audience penetration against the overall marketing objectives set during the early planning phases. If objectives are not being met, the marketing manager must find out why. It could be because of changes in the marketing environment, or it could be the result of a weak or ineffective marketing program. The marketing manager would look at the marketing plan more closely, starting from the present and working toward the beginning. Thus, the tactics are first evaluated and measured and then the strategy—TM, buyer behavior analysis, segmentation, objectives, MOA, situation analysis, and finally the overall mission or vision statements. The marketing manager must then make changes as needed. Education, experience, and lots of practice are the key ingredients for making effective changes in the marketing plan. The next section is a template for a marketing plan. Fill in each of the areas with the necessary information and data. At this point all relevant information will be useful. Remember you can always cut information that is considered useless or placed in the wrong categories.

A MARKETING PLAN TEMPLATE

For each of the following categories, please insert in Figure 1–2 all information that is essential to the marketing plan you're developing. More data and information are better than less. Feel free to attach additional pages as necessary to create a better plan. All the work can be done on either these or separate pages.

You now have a working marketing plan that serves as the basis for the IMC plan. The following chapters focus on the important job of developing an IMC plan that is synergistic and integrated with all other areas of marketing. The IMC planning also follows a commonsense flow; one such method is shown in chapter 2.

FIGURE 1–2 Marketing Plan Template

Company/Organization Mission:

Company/Organization Vision:

Situation Analysis:

History:

Environments served:

Market Opportunity Analysis (MOA):

Target Market:

Marketing Objectives:

   1.

   2.

   3.

   4.

   5.

Analysis of Buyer Behavior:

Market Segmentation Analysis:

Marketing Strategy:

Marketing Tactics:

   Product:

Price:

Channels of distribution:

IMC:

Marketing Program (Include Resource Allocations if Possible):

Response of the Target Market (Indicate How This Will Be Assessed or Accomplished):

Methods of Evaluation and Control:

CHAPTER

Planning for Integrated Marketing Communication

2

There is no one correct IMC plan. Every situation dictates a different method for getting the same results. The following plan, however, provides a good outline for the IMC planner. Feel free to follow it or to modify it to suit your needs. The plan should be developed by keeping your project at the top of your mind.

THE IMC MIX

As shown in Doc Ogden's Marketing Flowchart, IMC is one of the variables in the marketing mix. It is a tactical area, which requires tactical execution. Figure 2–1 shows the various areas of the IMC mix.

Each of the elements represents various aspects of the communication function of marketing. As a general rule, each of the functional areas can be defined as follows.

Advertising

Advertising is the development and execution of any *reminder, informational,* or *persuasive* message communicated to a targeted market or audience through a nonpersonal medium. The message is paid for, and the sponsor of the message or the product is identified. Most people would think of television, radio, or magazines as being traditional media; however, other media are available to an advertiser, such as newspapers, billboards (and other out-of-home media), flyers, and various direct vehicles. The key benefit of advertising is the ability to communicate to large numbers of people at the same time. In addition, advertising allows the advertisers to create continuity for a message. The messages sent to the large numbers of consumers are standardized, or uniform, because it is impossible to personalize a message for each consumer. Feedback from advertising comes in many forms, for example, product sales or awareness, votes for a candidate or issue, or a reduced number of smokers (for the heart or lung association). A key thing to remember is that advertising is not personal but rather impersonal.

Personal Selling

Personal selling is utilized to generate the benefits of one-to-one communication. Personal selling involves dialogue between the company and the consumer; that is, it is person-to-person (by telephone or face-to-face) communication between a buyer and a seller. Thus, personal selling has the advantage of persuasion. It allows the seller to respond directly to consumers' concerns and issues, as well as immediate feedback from a potential consumer. Obviously, personal selling only allows communication with a limited number of individuals per contact (usually one). This form of integrated marketing communication is also one of the most expensive methods per contact, whereas advertising offers a low cost per contact.

27

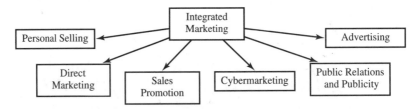

FIGURE 2–1 The Integrated Marketing Communication Mix

Sales Promotion

The object of sales promotion is to create, or induce, purchases. The buyer may be the final consumer, an intermediary, or an organization's own marketing staff. The major advantage of sales promotion is that it can develop a value-added package for the marketer. Incentives to purchase, or value additions, include coupons, free products or services, point-of-purchase displays (POPs), training programs, or free trips for top salespeople, to name a few. Sales promotions are those activities intended to induce purchases or to stimulate sales. Sales promotion activities supplement the other IMC mix variables of advertising, public relations and publicity, personal selling, and direct marketing. Sales promotions are indirect and nonpersonal and offer short-term stimulation. Some forms of promotion allow for semi-immediate feedback (e.g., coupons), although most do not. As in advertising, the sponsor of the message is identified. Costs per contact are higher than in advertising but lower than in personal selling (as a general rule). Costs associated with sales promotions vary greatly. Sales promotions are often tied to advertising, such as the inclusion of a coupon with a newspaper or magazine advertisement. Free samples of perfumes, often found in women's magazines, are also a tie-in between sales promotion and advertising.

Public Relations and Publicity

Although different activities, public relations and publicity are often grouped together because they perform the same function and are generally executed by the same individual, group, or department. **Publicity** utilizes the mass media, much the same as advertising. What makes it different is that it is not paid for in the traditional sense. Advertising pays for its medium, thereby giving it total control over the content and layout of the ad. Publicity utilizes unpaid media; thus it does not have total control over the content of the message, which is actually determined by the communications medium being utilized (TV station, newspaper, radio station, etc.). Publicity is considered to be "free," but it must be directed. There is a cost associated with the press releases issued by a given organization, which also involves persuasion by the director of this function. It should be noted that not all publicity is positive.

The act of publicity management is called **public relations.** It is up to the marketers to create and place various press releases and interviews to establish a favorable organizational image. In addition, the public relations personnel must develop a course of action and a timetable for the release of publicity and weigh its effectiveness and cost efficiency. With public relations and publicity, the organization must be *proactive* rather than *reactive* when responding to its markets and environments.

Direct Marketing

Until very recently, not a lot of attention was paid to direct marketing. In fact, it was considered a "specialty" form of traditional marketing and often fell under advertising. The Direct Marketing Association (DMA), in its *Fact Book on Direct Response Mar-*

keting (1982), defines direct marketing as *an interactive system of marketing that uses one or more advertising media to effect a measurable response and/or transaction at any location.* Direct marketing allows for personalized communication. In addition, it can be utilized with many different media or with just one. For example, direct mail can be used alone to reach the targeted market or it can accompany TV advertising. Direct marketing looks to create an immediate response, as well as a measurable response, from the market. Various forms of direct marketing include but are not limited to direct mail, telemarketing, direct selling, and direct-response advertising. With the rise in expenditures for traditional advertising media (especially television), marketers look for other methods of reaching their targeted markets at a more reasonable cost. Because of advances in database management, many targeted customers can be reached through direct marketing in a less expensive manner than television advertising. In addition, direct marketing is measurable, so the organization knows exactly how effective its marketing was. Direct marketing stimulates an immediate response and thus is a growing area of IMC. One must manage the direct marketing functions to ensure that they're integrated with all other marketing communication areas.

Cybermarketing

Many methods of marketing and advertising utilize the computer and computer networks such as the World Wide Web (WWW). Together, these methods are known as **cybermarketing.** The basic function or objective of cybermarketing is to use the power of online networks, computer communications, and digital interactive media to reach target audiences or to enhance marketing or integrated marketing communications. Some of the various types of cybermarketing are CD-ROM (compact disc–read only memory); E-mail, electronic data interchange (EDI), and business-oriented database services; posting, hosting, or presenting information on the Internet; and online marketing research. Why would the IMC planner wish to engage in cybermarketing? Cybermarketing often provides an inexpensive alternative to traditional media (e.g., brochures, product sheets, and catalogs), which can be time-intensive in terms of revisions, mistakes, and so on. Also, some traditional media have a hit-or-miss quality (telephone "tag," direct mail, etc.). Cybermarketing does add more interactivity for the IMC planner and the campaign, but it does not fix all of the problems associated with traditional marketing. What cybermarketing may do is reduce a dependence on paper, add more information (especially for high-tech products or products new to the marketplace), and take away traditional media barriers. More information about cybermarketing is provided later.

THE IMC PLAN

An understanding of the IMC mix is essential in putting together an effective and creative IMC plan. Given an understanding of marketing and how important integration is in a marketing program, one can put together an IMC plan that will overwhelm the competition. In the process of effectively developing and implementing an IMC plan, the marketers and advertisers should always follow the marketing concept. Consumers' wants and needs should always be the main focus of the program. To lose this focus means that the program, although creative or award-winning, will sell no product or service. There are numerous ways to develop an IMC campaign. Just as on a directional map, there are many routes to the desired destination. There are no perfect outlines to fit every IMC manager's needs. The flowchart in Figure 2–2 offers direction based on clarity, content, and simplicity.

IMC Mission and Vision Statement

When developing a mission and vision statement, the IMC manager must look to the marketing plan. Quite simply, a *mission statement* tells why the organization is in business, and this translates into the reason for having IMC. What is the overall purpose? Why does this function exist? If the manager doesn't know the reason for having a department or division, how could he possibly communicate this function to the targeted customers? A *vision statement,* on the other hand, should answer the question, "What do we want to develop or create?" The vision should capture a picture of where the organization sees itself in the future. More specifically, the vision should create the ideal image the department wants to provide. The vision statement should be developed using an integrated approach, and it should be a shared vision. In other words, all individuals affected by the vision should have input into its development.

The vision should instill a goal. It should create excitement and teamwork among those affected by it. While in the process of creating the vision, information should be gleaned from the marketing plan. What is the overall marketing mission, as well as the organizational mission? In developing these mission and vision statements, data from the marketing and the IMC situational analysis should be utilized. Some of the bene-

FIGURE 2–2 Doc Ogden's Integrated Marketing Communication Flowchart

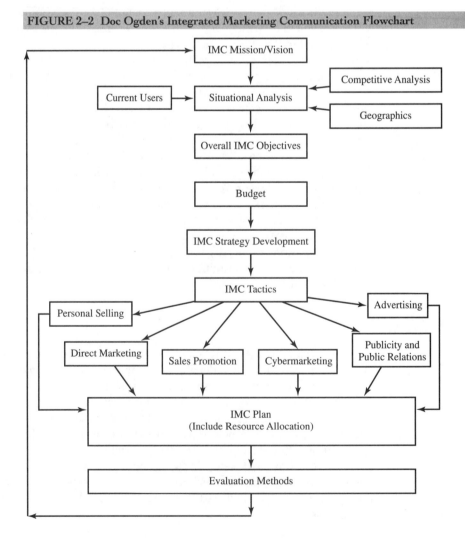

fits of a shared mission and vision statement could include (but are not limited by) the following:

- Stakeholders become aware of why the IMC exists and where it is headed.
- A measurement tool is utilized that workers can use to increase their self-worth and at the same time promote the organization.
- All IMC activities are developed from a common plan, and workers understand what creations are needed and wanted.
- All jobs are connected by a common purpose.

Indirectly, those involved have the chance to work for something that they believe in and that they had a part in developing. A byproduct is increased creativity, innovation, and risk taking. In other words, the shared mission and vision of the IMC planner provides inspiration and a destination that all members of the IMC team can share.

Situational Analysis

Whereas the situational analysis of the company or organization provides the big overview of the company as a whole, the IMC situational analysis provides a history of the IMC functions and an assessment of the environment in which IMC managers must work. Several factors must be considered in the situational analysis. The company or organization that the IMC plan is being created for must be analyzed. A product and service history and evaluation should be included. The competition, geographics, and current consumers should all be analyzed. For example, what and who make up the targeted audience? A listing of the strengths and weakness of the product or service can be added to help strengthen the analysis. Specifically, a SWOT (**s**trengths/**w**eaknesses/**o**pportunities/**t**hreats) analysis could be performed, resulting in a "problems and opportunities" graph.

The situational analysis section lends itself perfectly to the use of figures, charts, graphs, and tables. Use these tools whenever possible to shorten the written report. Remember, an ideal IMC plan is not too long (50–60 pages maximum), but at the same time it must contain all the essential data in the proper development of an overall IMC campaign.

The company analysis should include as much of the following data as possible:

- Sales and profit figures
- Company mission and vision
- Company orientation—risk taking or conservative
- Corporate (or organizational) resources, including but not limited to financial, technological, and human
- Aggressiveness
- Market share
- Sales trends

In addition, the following information will be very useful in developing an effective, innovative, and creative IMC plan:

- What are the various environments (social, political, technological, cultural, economic, natural, etc.) that may affect the company and its IMC execution?
- Within the industry, what have been the overall trends in sales?
- Within the industry, what have been the overall trends in market share?
- What are the industrial marketing practices?
- Are major events forthcoming that will have an effect on the product or service?

This should be an in-depth yet brief analysis. Appendix A lists a number of sources for generating the answers to the preceding questions.

Product (or service) history (analysis) should address the question, "What do the consumers want and/or need?" A lot of the data needed may be found within the company itself. In addition, the marketing plan is an excellent place to begin looking for the information necessary for an outstanding and creative IMC plan. As stated earlier, the IMC should be synonymous with integration. It is important for the IMC manager and planner to have an understanding of how all the marketing mix variables fit together. No decisions should be made in a vacuum. There needs to be an integration, not only of the marketing communications, but also of the marketing mix variables (product, price, channels of distribution, and IMC). The following pieces of information are necessary to develop an effective product analysis:

- Product or service background
- Current problems facing the product, brand, or service
- Past IMC or advertising themes
- Past IMC budgets
- Past to present media spending
- Current slogan, tag line, copy position, and so on

In addition, there should be a product evaluation, which includes but is not limited to the answers to the following questions:

- What is the quality of the product?
- What is the total product concept, including the physical product or service; the benefits offered by the product; the needs and wants satisfiers of the product; and the packaging, labeling, and branding?
- What has been added to or deleted from the product or service over the past five years?
- Have there been new markets for the product?
- Have there been any new uses for the product?
- How do intermediaries (i.e., wholesalers and retailers) feel about the product or service?
- Is distribution effective? What type of distribution system is utilized? Is there intensive, selective, or exclusive distribution?
- How is product service?
- Is the brand name well known?
- What problems do consumers see with the product? Can these problems be addressed and/or corrected?
- What features and benefits of the product are unique? Are there features that are different than those of the competition to allow for adequate product differentiation? Specifically, how is product differentiation achieved (if at all)?
- How do the consumers perceive the product (i.e., high-tech, old-fashioned, modern)?
- Are product users satisfied?
- What are the return policies?
- What are the warranties and guarantees?
- What are the product sizes? Is the product packaged to be user friendly?

These are some of the things that should go into this section. Each situation, however, dictates the need for either more or less information. The idea is to develop a brand identity, or *brand personality*. Products or brands should be discussed and addressed in terms of their *attributes, functions, and personalities*. The physical features of the brand generally are referred to as attributes, the psychological features are the personality, and the functions tend to be a combination of physical and psychological features. Much of the information about the product must be gathered through product research; thus, a great deal of consumer testing needs to be done in order to generate the data necessary to answer a number of the questions addressed here. Appendix B offers techniques that can be utilized to provide data to the product researcher.

Competitive analyses are helpful to fully understand in what industry the product or service is really competing. The planner also needs to know how, why, and when the competition will respond to changes in IMC tactics and executions. Products that compete directly as well as indirectly should be included in the analysis, with emphasis on direct competition. The following list should be helpful in generating an in-depth competitive analysis:

1. Direct competition
2. Indirect competition
3. IMC strengths and weaknesses
4. A history of IMC themes utilized by the competition (include the current theme)
5. IMC effectiveness
6. A history of competitive IMC expenditures. This section could (and probably should) be broken down into the various IMC mix variables (i.e., personal selling, sales promotion, advertising, direct marketing, public relations and publicity, cyber-marketing)
7. Hard data on the effectiveness of all past and current IMC programs developed and executed by the competition
8. Strengths and weaknesses of competitive products, brands, lines, and so on
9. Indications of the acceptance by the trade of any IMC programs, both current and past
10. Specific media placement practices of the main competition

Many of the sources shown in appendix A will be useful in securing data for this section of the situational analysis. In addition, the following sources may help generate competitive data.

1. Directories
    a. The *Million Dollar Directory: Leading Public and Private Companies* is published by Dun & Bradstreet and offers brief summaries of over 150,000 U.S. companies. The information is based on SIC (Standard Industrial Classification) codes, thus allowing access to a particular industry.
    b. The *Encyclopedia of Associations* lists information on numerous (around 22,000) U.S. and worldwide organizations. The IMC researcher should pay particular attention to the listings of trade and professional organizations.
    c. *Brands and Their Companies and Companies and Their Brands* is a directory that provides limited information on specific brands by company.
    d. *The Thomas Register.*
    e. *Conover-Mast Purchasing Directory.*
2. Miscellaneous Sources
    a. The United States Bureau of the Census publications.
        (1) The Census of Transportation
        (2) The Census of Population
        (3) The Census of Mineral Industries
        (4) The Census of Agribusiness
        (5) The Census of Retail Trade
        (6) The Census of Wholesale Trade
        (7) The Census of Service Industries

       (8) "The Census of Manufacturers" (also "The Annual Survey of Manufacturers")
       (9) "The Census of Housing"
  b. *Encyclopedia of Business Information Resources*
  c. *Wasserman's Statistics Sources*
  d. *Statistical Abstract of the United States*
  e. *County and City Data Book*
  f. *County Business Patterns*

    Geographics (or market analysis) is undertaken to help the IMC planner understand which geographic areas are key, either because of the strong position the advertiser enjoys in the area or because of the problems associated with doing business in a particular geographic area. In addition, the data gathered in the market analysis provide the media planners with geographic information that facilitates media buys and dollar allocation (budgets). Much of the data gathered in the market analysis can be directly utilized in the consumer evaluation; for that matter, the data gathered for any purpose of the IMC or marketing plan may be generalizable to another section. Product usage data, which are important in developing a geographic analysis, indicate the current number of product users and the amount of products utilized. Although these data can be somewhat hard to obtain, the following commercial sources do supply them to companies and advertisers: Nielsen's *SCANTRACK,* IRI's *InfoScan,* and to some extent Nielsen's *Food and Drug Index.*

    Another method of analyzing the geographic area is through the use of indexing. Indexes are created to provide a "best-guess" estimate of a market's potential for product sales. The indexes can also show how well a product, brand, or service is performing in a given market. The two major indexes are the **brand development index (BDI)** and the **category development index (CDI).** These two indexes, which are calculated by using information from varying sources, indicate how well a particular brand is performing in a given market. Scores above 100, which is the standard score benchmark, or the average, indicate that a product or brand is doing well in the market. Scores below 100 indicate that the brand is not performing well in the market (compared to the other geographic markets).

    One of the main reasons for an above-average brand performance is the market itself. The generic market for a product category may be lifting the score of the brand. To understand the market's support of a particular product category, a CDI can be calculated. As is the case with BDI indexes, a score over 100 shows that the market is receptive to the brand category. If the market doesn't utilize the product category as much as the other markets, the score will be below 100 (100 being the benchmark, or average, for the product categories). The researcher should also compare the BDI with the CDI. If the BDI is lower than the CDI and both indexes have a score over 100, the brand and the product category are doing well but the specific brand is not performing as well as the other competing brands on the market. BDIs and CDIs can be calculated by utilizing the following formulas:

$$\frac{\% \text{ of a brand's total U.S. sales in a market}}{\% \text{ of total U.S. population in a market}} \times 100 = BDI$$

$$\frac{\% \text{ of a category's total U.S. sales in a market}}{\% \text{ of total U.S. population in a market}} \times 100 = CDI$$

Sales and Marketing Management (S & MM) puts out a publication entitled *Survey of Buying Power* (usually in its August issue). The survey of buying power provides statistics on the United States, individual states, standard metropolitan statistical areas (MSAs), counties, and large cities. The data include population figures, households, and effective buying income (EBI) for each of the areas. In addition, there are data on six categories of retail sales. *S & MM* also publishes the *Survey of Media Markets,* which offers statistics on geographical areas that Arbitron calls *designated market areas* (DMAs). The buying power index (BPI) can be calculated from data gleaned from *S & MM's Survey of Buying Power.* The index allows the planner or researcher to identify potential sales for a given market by looking at the consumer's buying power. Although it is recommended that the IMC planner actually secure a copy of the *Survey of Buying Power,* Figure 2–3 illustrates how a BPI is calculated.

Mediamark Research, Inc. (MRI) and the Simmons Market Research Bureau (SMRB) also provide data on product usage by broad geographical categories. These indexes allow the IMC specialist to project sales potential for a given geographic area. Figure 2–4 shows a sample page from the SMRB that illustrates how it can be used by the IMC planner in a geographic analysis.

A current users evaluation is necessary to understand how, why, when, and who buys an organization's products and/or services. It is important to put together an in-depth profile of the typical consumer, for the advertiser. The IMC planners should be able to picture the "typical" customer in order to turn the advertising into reality. To develop such a picture, a number of pieces of information and data are required. The following list should help to provide an accurate picture of who the consumer really is. These items should be included in the consumer evaluation.

1. **Demographics,** *variables,* are measurable characteristics of the population as a whole. Demographics allow for the segmentation of markets and ease the process of buying media. Demographic variables would include but not necessarily be limited to the following:
   a. Occupation
   b. Marital status
   c. Household income
   d. Education
   e. Social class
   f. Age
   g. Head of household
   h. Race
   i. Family size
   j. Family life-cycle
2. **Psychographics** are bits of *life-style analysis;* that is, what consumers do. Psychographics can be generated by performing an AIO (**a**ctivities, **i**nterests, and **o**pinions) analysis. In addition, IMC managers can utilize VALS data (VALS = Values and Lifestyles), if available.
3. **Geodemographics** are a combination of demographics and psychographics (or life-style characteristics). Generally these data are developed for small groups of consumers within a given geographic boundary. Consumers that share certain psychographic and demographic profiles tend to live in geographic proximity to one another.
4. **Behavioristics** deal with information on what drives consumers to make purchases. Issues like social influences, attitudes about product quality, solutions to consumer problems, brand loyalty, consumer awareness of products, and other outside

Sales & Marketing Management's patented Buying Power Index, or BPI, has been a part of the *Survey of Buying Power* for more than 30 years, providing marketers with a standardized measurement of the relative buying power of states, metros, counties, and cities. The BPI listed in the Survey's data sections is a general indicator constructed from data on total population, total Effective Buying Income (EBI), and total retail sales—the three basic categories of statistics covered by the *Survey*.

For those who need to define their markets more specifically, however, it is possible to construct a customized version of the BPI, using any of the subclassifications of statistics in the *Survey*'s three basic data fields. By selecting a Demographic component (population), an Economic component (income), and a Distribution component (retail sales), you can use the formula outlined below to convert data from individual markets into a custom BPI for your product or service.

For our purposes, we will label these three BPI components as follows: Demographic = **A**; Economic = **B**; and Distribution = **C**. Looking at each of these areas individually, here's how you might go about selecting them:

A: Demographic—First of all, you'll need to isolate the population or household-related factor that best describes your "ideal" consumer. For example, if you're selling video games, the 18-and-under age segment is a better indicator of market potential than total population. On the other hand, if your product is media oriented (magazines, mail-order catalogs, etc.), you may want to use household counts as your demographic component.

B: Economic—The next step involves selecting the income group(s) best suited to your product. Here, the *Survey* offers you five basic ranges of household incomes, and you can easily combine two or more groups to achieve a broader spectrum of potential. For example, if you're selling a premium-priced product, you might select households with incomes of $35,000 and above.

C: Distribution—Isolating a particular store group that parallels your preferred channel of distribution is the final step in the preliminary selection process. If you're selling beer, for example, you may want to combine Eating & Drinking Place sales and Food Store sales, since these are the two largest markets for your product. On the other hand, if you're selling shampoo, Drugstores and General Merchandise stores (which includes department stores and discount stores) would be a better distribution-related indicator.

Once these three factors have been selected, you can then compute your custom BPI by following this simple four step process:

Step 1—For each market (region, state, metro, county, etc.), you'll first need to compare local activity to that for the U.S. as a whole, producing a ratio for each of the three BPI factors (A-B-C). In this example, the Demographic component (A) would be calculated as follows:

$$\frac{\text{Market's Pop. Under 18}}{\text{U.S. Pop. Under 18}} = X\%$$

Next, using households with EBIs of $35,000 and above as the Economic factor (B), we compare the market with the appropriate U.S. total:

$$\frac{\text{Market's Hshlds. w/EBIs } \$35,000+}{\text{U.S. Hshlds. w/EBIs } \$35,000+} = Y\%$$

And finally, we calculate the Distribution component (C) by constructing a ratio of local Food Store sales to U.S. Food Store sales:

$$\frac{\text{Market's Food Store Sales}}{\text{U.S. Food Store Sales}} = Z\%$$

Step 2—Armed with these percentages (X-Y-Z), we are now ready to assign weights to the demographic, economic, and distribution-related components, according to their perceived importance in the selling process. In all cases, the assigned weights should be expressed in decimals (50% = .5, 30% = .3, etc.).

Since income is often cited as the most important indicator of potential purchasing power, your weighting of these factors might look something like this:

Factor **A** (Demographic)—.2 (20%)
Factor **B** (Economic)—.5 (50%)
Factor **C** (Distribution)—.3 (30%)

Step 3—Multiplying each component ratio (X-Y-Z) by its appropriate weight and adding the resulting totals will then give you the BPI for a particular market:

$$(.2 \times X\%) + (.5 \times Y\%) + (.3 \times Z\%) = \text{BPI}$$

The fractional figure you arrive at can then be used as a relative indicator to compare the potential buying power of this market to that for the U.S. as a whole (U.S. = 100.0000).*

Step 4—Repeat this same procedure for each targeted market, compiling a list of markets ranked according to their BPIs. If your particular product warrants the construction of a BPI with only two factors (or possibly four or five), remember that the same principles apply in terms of weighting the various components. In other words, the percentages should still total 100%, regardless of the number of BPI components.

*Note: *If you're selling your product in a limited number of markets, you may want to substitute the combined total of these markets for the U.S. totals in your calculations. In such a case, your BPI of 100.0000 would represent the total of these markets only.*

FIGURE 2–3 How to Construct a Custom BPI

Courtesy of Sales and Marketing Management. Used with permission of Bill Communication, Ny, Ny.

influences that may have an impact on consumers' behavior need to be addressed. In short, the current consumer evaluation should include all relevant data and information about current users and prospective users. Appendix C offers various sources of data about consumers that are available to the IMC planner.

The whole idea around the development of a situational analysis is to find information that will be helpful to the execution of the IMC campaign. The culmination of the situational analysis should be a further definition of the **targeted market.** The IMC planner should identify a typical consumer toward whom the IMC executions should be aimed. This target market must match the overall marketing targeted market but will probably be better defined. Certainly, among other things, the target market needs to include the four "ics" (demographics, geographics, psychographics, and behavioristics), as well as product usage behavior, needs and wants, expectations, problems, opportunities, and strengths and weaknesses. Having defined the targeted market is some detail, we now address the next phase of the IMC plan—setting objectives.

Overall IMC Objectives

Objectives are simply goals, things that need to be accomplished, and milestones that need to be reached. The IMC objectives can be taken from the marketing plan. Usually the clients or marketing managers have specific items that they want to be achieved. Generally, these goals—for sales, profits, market share, or margins—are for the period of time covered in the IMC campaign. For the most part, the objectives are developed from the situational analysis, specifically from the opportunities that were outlined there. Thus, the objectives should be logical deductions from the marketing plan and situational analysis.

The objectives will be used as an evaluation tool. At the end of the campaign, the IMC manager can look back to see if the desired results were achieved. If they weren't, the manager needs to know why. Changes can be made to better achieve the objectives, or objectives that were unachievable can be changed. All in all, objectives provide direction to the campaign planner. Specific criteria need to be applied to the process of setting objectives, and the following list is a guideline:

- The objectives must be **measurable** and **quantifiable.** In other words, the objectives must be written in such a way as to allow for measurement at the end of the campaign. The objectives were either achieved or they weren't.
- The objectives must specify **who** the **target audience** is, **when** the set goals should be accomplished (a time line), and **what** specifically should be accomplished.
- The objectives must be **realistic.** If the goal cannot be achieved, it is useless to include it in the objectives. Unrealistic objectives have a negative effect on the personnel that have been assigned to carry out the project.
- The objectives must be **clear.** All individuals involved in the campaign must be striving for the same goals.
- The objectives must be **integrated.** All components of the marketing and integrated marketing communications areas must have goals that are common to the overall marketing objectives. It would be useless to have a communication goal of "friendliness toward consumers" while at the same time reducing the number of service providers.

In addition, all elements of the marketing communication mix must have overall objectives stated as part of the IMC plan. Each IMC mix variable will develop its own specific goals, which will help to achieve the advertiser's or marketer's overall objectives. A sample goal may read something like this: "To increase market share of Bob's Burger World by 3 percent in the top 10 ADIs during the next one-year campaign."

FIGURE 2–4 Theme Parks (Including Water Parks) — Parks Attended in Last 12 Months (Males)

	TOTAL U.S. '000	ATTENDED THEME PARK A '000	B % DOWN	C % ACROSS	D INDX	BUSCH GARDENS A '000	B % DOWN	C % ACROSS	D INDX	DISNEYLAND A '000	B % DOWN	C % ACROSS	D INDX	DISNEYWORLD/EPCOT A '000	B % DOWN	C % ACROSS	D INDX
TOTAL	86476	18372	100.0	21.2	100	2254	100.0	2.6	100	3376	100.0	3.9	100	3701	100.0	4.3	100
OUTDOOR QUINTILE 1	17345	4337	23.6	25.0	118	*408	18.1	2.4	90	1128	33.4	6.5	167	902	24.4	5.2	122
QUINTILE 2	17500	3967	21.6	22.7	107	416	18.5	2.4	91	686	20.3	3.9	100	781	21.1	4.5	104
QUINTILE 3	16975	3445	18.8	20.3	96	*436	19.3	2.6	99	508	15.0	3.0	77	607	16.4	3.6	84
QUINTILE 4	17896	3521	19.2	19.7	93	562	24.9	3.1	120	598	17.7	3.3	86	726	19.6	4.1	95
QUINTILE 5	16760	3102	16.9	18.5	87	*433	19.2	2.6	99	*456	13.5	2.7	70	685	18.5	4.1	95
RADIO-DRIVE TIME QUINTILE 1	15919	3736	20.3	23.5	110	584	25.9	3.7	141	707	20.9	4.4	114	968	26.2	6.1	142
QUINTILE 2	16650	3851	21.0	23.1	109	*392	17.4	2.4	90	685	20.3	4.1	105	655	17.7	3.9	92
QUINTILE 3	18472	3640	19.8	19.7	93	*446	19.8	2.4	93	536	15.9	2.9	74	704	19.0	3.8	89
QUINTILE 4	17502	3960	21.6	22.6	106	487	21.6	2.8	107	683	20.2	3.9	100	714	19.3	4.1	95
QUINTILE 5	17933	3186	17.3	17.8	84	*345	15.3	1.9	74	765	22.7	4.3	109	660	17.8	3.7	86
RADIO-MID-DAY TERCILE 1	22274	4951	26.9	22.2	105	574	25.5	2.6	99	842	24.9	3.8	97	1007	27.2	4.5	106
TERCILE 2	22690	4785	26.0	21.1	99	727	32.3	3.2	123	828	24.5	3.6	93	826	22.3	3.6	85
TERCILE 3	41512	8636	47.0	20.8	98	953	42.3	2.3	88	1706	50.5	4.1	105	1869	50.5	4.5	105
RADIO-TOTAL QUINTILE 1	17652	4167	22.7	23.6	111	592	26.3	3.4	129	724	21.4	4.1	105	911	24.6	5.2	121
QUINTILE 2	17803	3731	20.3	21.0	99	*380	16.9	2.1	82	684	20.3	3.8	98	610	16.5	3.4	80
QUINTILE 3	17018	3634	19.8	21.4	101	474	21.0	2.8	107	566	16.8	3.3	85	750	20.3	4.4	103
QUINTILE 4	16696	3684	20.1	22.1	104	506	22.4	3.0	116	784	23.2	4.7	120	773	20.9	4.6	108
QUINTILE 5	17308	3156	17.2	18.2	86	*302	13.4	1.7	67	618	18.3	3.6	91	658	17.8	3.8	89
TV-PRIME TIME QUINTILE 1	17447	3503	19.1	20.1	95	*538	23.9	3.1	118	743	22.0	4.3	109	745	20.1	4.3	100
QUINTILE 2	17086	3469	18.9	20.3	96	*422	18.7	2.5	95	627	18.6	3.7	94	702	19.0	4.1	96
QUINTILE 3	17399	3740	20.4	21.5	101	*455	20.2	2.6	100	650	19.3	3.7	96	912	24.6	5.2	122
QUINTILE 4	17788	3800	20.7	21.4	101	*345	15.3	1.9	74	665	19.7	3.7	96	531	14.3	3.0	70
QUINTILE 5	16755	3861	21.0	23.0	108	495	22.0	3.0	113	691	20.5	4.1	106	812	21.9	4.8	113
TV-DAYTIME TERCILE 1	24355	4914	26.7	20.2	95	718	31.9	2.9	113	1160	34.4	4.8	122	876	23.7	3.6	84
TERCILE 2	23853	5288	28.8	22.2	104	661	29.3	2.8	106	830	24.6	3.5	89	1036	28.0	4.3	101
TERCILE 3	38268	8170	44.5	21.3	100	875	38.8	2.3	88	1387	41.1	3.6	93	1789	48.3	4.7	109
TV-TOTAL QUINTILE 1	17275	3326	18.1	19.3	91	*539	23.9	3.1	120	830	24.6	4.8	123	623	16.8	3.6	84
QUINTILE 2	17758	3699	20.1	20.8	98	454	20.1	2.6	98	682	20.2	3.8	98	635	17.2	3.6	84
QUINTILE 3	17287	3789	20.6	21.9	103	*363	16.1	2.1	81	559	16.6	3.2	83	804	21.7	4.6	109
QUINTILE 4	17396	3704	20.2	21.3	100	523	23.2	3.0	115	557	16.5	3.2	82	808	21.8	4.6	109
QUINTILE 5	16760	3853	21.0	23.0	108	376	16.7	2.2	86	748	22.2	4.5	114	831	22.5	5.0	116
YELLOW PAGES QUINTILE 1	19295	5568	30.3	28.9	136	732	32.5	3.8	146	729	21.6	3.8	97	961	26.0	5.0	116
QUINTILE 2	13122	3426	18.6	26.1	123	634	28.1	4.8	185	647	19.2	4.9	126	670	18.1	5.1	119
QUINTILE 3	12773	2671	14.5	20.9	98	*215	9.5	1.7	65	*351	10.4	2.7	70	687	18.6	5.4	126
QUINTILE 4	19241	4039	22.0	21.0	99	503	22.3	2.6	100	960	28.4	5.0	128	1082	29.2	5.6	131
QUINTILE 5	22046	2668	14.5	12.1	57	**170	7.5	0.8	30	690	20.4	3.1	80	*300	8.1	1.4	32

	Total	'000	%	%	Index	'000	%	%	Index	'000	%	%	Index	'000	%	%	Index
MAGAZINES-NEWSPAPERS: DUAL	19667	5065	27.6	25.8	121	595	26.4	3.0	116	998	29.6	5.1	130	1012	27.3	5.1	120
MAGAZINE IMPERATIVE	17170	3608	19.6	21.0	99	*371	16.5	2.2	83	666	19.7	3.9	99	596	16.1	3.5	81
NEWSPAPER IMPERATIVE	29982	6309	34.3	21.0	99	789	35.0	2.6	101	1095	32.4	3.7	94	1448	39.1	4.8	113
MAGAZINES-OUTDOOR: DUAL	16461	4323	23.5	26.3	124	*390	17.3	2.4	91	932	27.6	5.7	145	800	21.6	4.9	114
MAGAZINE IMPERATIVE	21887	4773	26.0	21.8	103	630	28.0	2.9	110	683	20.2	4.0	103	988	26.7	4.5	105
OUTDOOR IMPERATIVE	30283	6331	34.5	20.9	98	753	33.4	2.5	95	1218	36.1	4.0	103	1350	36.5	4.5	104
MAGAZINES-RADIO: DUAL	16688	3905	21.3	23.4	110	*375	16.6	2.2	86	637	18.9	3.8	98	678	18.3	4.1	95
MAGAZINE IMPERATIVE	21675	5138	28.0	23.7	112	613	27.2	2.8	109	1034	30.6	4.8	122	1072	29.0	4.9	116
RADIO IMPERATIVE	30143	6250	34.0	20.7	98	877	38.9	2.9	112	1109	32.8	3.7	94	1299	35.1	4.3	101
MAGAZINES-TELEVISION: DUAL	14526	3513	19.1	24.2	114	*403	17.9	2.8	106	872	25.8	6.0	154	703	19.0	4.8	113
MAGAZINE IMPERATIVE	23736	5820	31.7	24.5	115	650	28.6	2.7	105	900	26.7	3.8	97	1188	32.1	5.0	117
TELEVISION IMPERATIVE	31506	5798	31.6	18.4	87	825	36.6	2.6	100	1003	29.7	3.2	82	1003	27.1	3.2	74
MAGAZINES-YELLOW PGS: DUAL	14760	4090	22.3	27.7	130	473	21.0	3.2	123	606	18.0	4.1	105	756	20.4	5.1	120
MAGAZINE IMPERATIVE	23644	4656	25.3	19.7	93	469	20.8	3.2	76	1082	32.0	3.6	93	1025	27.7	5.1	101
YELLOW PGS IMPERATIVE	26117	6438	35.0	24.7	116	1025	45.5	3.9	151	950	28.1	3.6	93	1307	35.3	5.0	117
NEWSPAPERS-OUTDOOR: DUAL	19474	4825	26.3	24.8	117	647	28.7	3.3	127	812	24.1	4.2	107	970	26.2	5.0	116
NEWSPAPER IMPERATIVE	28734	6014	32.7	21.0	99	776	34.4	2.7	104	994	29.4	3.5	89	1396	37.7	4.9	114
OUTDOOR IMPERATIVE	24817	5210	28.4	21.0	99	*370	16.4	1.5	57	1221	36.2	4.9	126	988	26.7	4.0	93
NEWSPAPERS-RADIO: DUAL	19351	4775	26.0	24.7	116	650	28.8	3.4	129	801	23.7	4.2	106	1014	27.4	5.1	122
NEWSPAPER IMPERATIVE	28814	6422	35.0	22.3	105	774	34.3	2.7	103	1211	35.9	4.2	108	1482	40.0	5.1	120
RADIO IMPERATIVE	24996	5043	27.4	20.2	95	531	23.6	2.1	82	921	27.3	3.7	94	777	21.0	3.1	73
NEWSPAPER-TELEVISION: DUAL	18257	4041	22.0	22.1	104	535	23.7	2.9	112	784	23.2	4.3	110	845	22.8	5.6	108
NEWSPAPER IMPERATIVE	30206	7224	39.3	23.1	113	797	35.4	2.6	101	1113	33.0	3.8	98	1686	45.6	5.6	130
TELEVISION IMPERATIVE	25588	4683	25.5	18.3	86	600	26.6	2.3	90	974	28.9	3.8	98	745	20.1	2.9	68
NEWSPAPERS-YELLOW PGS: DUAL	18853	5177	28.2	27.5	129	673	29.9	3.6	137	737	21.8	3.9	100	1085	29.3	5.8	134
NEWSPAPER IMPERATIVE	30100	5792	31.5	19.2	91	642	28.5	3.6	82	1220	36.1	4.0	104	1412	38.2	4.7	110
YELLOW PGS IMPERATIVE	20133	5037	27.4	25.0	118	778	34.5	3.9	148	814	24.1	4.0	104	496	21.5	4.0	92
OUTDOOR-RADIO: DUAL	17665	4135	22.5	23.4	110	461	20.5	2.6	100	880	26.1	5.0	128	858	23.2	4.9	113
OUTDOOR IMPERATIVE	27313	5895	32.1	21.6	102	583	25.9	2.1	82	1270	37.6	4.6	119	1197	32.3	4.4	102
RADIO IMPERATIVE	27651	5789	31.5	20.9	99	852	37.8	3.1	118	758	22.5	2.7	70	1119	30.2	4.0	95
OUTDOOR-TELEVISION: DUAL	17314	3841	20.9	22.2	104	*354	15.7	2.5	95	969	28.7	5.6	143	633	17.1	3.7	85
OUTDOOR IMPERATIVE	27475	6615	36.0	24.1	113	678	30.1	3.0	95	1154	34.2	4.2	108	1496	40.4	4.0	127
TELEVISION IMPERATIVE	28407	5317	28.9	18.7	88	807	35.8	2.8	85	847	25.1	3.0	76	1036	28.0	3.6	85
OUTDOOR-YELLOW PGS: DUAL	16469	4781	26.0	29.0	137	544	24.1	3.3	127	842	24.9	5.4	131	965	26.1	5.9	137
OUTDOOR IMPERATIVE	28801	5212	28.4	18.1	85	453	20.1	1.6	60	1273	37.7	4.4	113	1087	29.4	3.8	88
YELLOW PGS IMPERATIVE	23305	5714	31.1	24.5	115	953	42.3	4.1	157	732	21.7	3.1	80	1117	30.2	4.8	112
RADIO-TELEVISION: DUAL	17443	3842	20.9	22.0	104	*508	22.5	2.9	112	636	18.8	3.6	93	594	16.0	3.4	80
RADIO IMPERATIVE	28325	6459	35.2	22.8	107	740	32.8	2.6	100	1063	31.5	3.8	96	1378	37.2	4.9	114
TELEVISION IMPERATIVE	27576	5356	29.2	19.4	91	675	29.9	2.4	94	1130	33.5	4.1	105	1132	30.6	4.1	96
RADIO-YELLOW PGS: DUAL	16701	4490	24.4	26.9	127	691	30.7	4.1	159	757	22.4	4.5	116	987	26.7	5.5	138
RADIO IMPERATIVE	28945	5158	28.1	17.8	84	493	21.9	1.7	65	1027	30.4	3.5	91	996	26.9	3.4	80
YELLOW PGS IMPERATIVE	23189	5884	32.0	25.4	119	813	36.1	3.5	135	824	24.4	3.6	91	1052	28.4	4.5	106
TELEVISION-YELLOW PGS: DUAL	15038	3958	21.5	26.3	124	666	29.5	4.4	170	663	19.6	4.4	113	670	18.1	4.5	104
ELEVISION IMPERATIVE	30626	4822	26.2	15.7	74	467	20.7	1.5	59	1255	37.2	4.1	105	980	26.5	3.2	75
YELLOW PAGES IMPERATIVE	25327	6671	36.3	26.3	124	846	37.5	3.3	128	834	24.7	3.3	84	1371	37.0	5.4	126

SIMMONS MARKET RESEARCH BUREAU, INC. 1990

*PROJECTION RELATIVELY UNSTABLE BECAUSE OF SAMPLE BASE—USE WITH CAUTION

**NUMBER OF CASES TOO SMALL FOR RELIABILITY—SHOWN FOR CONSISTENCY ONLY

Budget

Although a very important decision, budgeting is often the most neglected part of the IMC plan. The idea of budgeting is to decide what amount of money will be needed to best achieve the IMC objectives. In other words, what is the "right" amount of money that should be spent. Too much spending ends up in wasted dollars, whereas not enough translates to loss of sales and market share. A number of techniques are used in budgeting, and the most popular are discussed here.

1. **Percentage-of-sales method.** In using this method, the budgeter simply allots a percentage amount for each brand, product, or service based on past or forecasted sales. For example, a company with sales of $1 million decides it needs to spend 2 percent on IMC. This translates to a budgeted amount, per product, of $20,000. Although easy to develop and administer, there are some problems associated with this method. It increases advertising dollar amounts when sales go up or are expected to go up. What happens to a new product with few sales? Also, if there is a recessionary period, sales generally go down. If sales go down, advertising dollars also decline. In this situation, it may be wiser to increase advertising amounts to generate additional market share and sales rather than letting the advertising or IMC functions have less money. Thus, this method is generally used in combination with one or two of the other methods to allow for changes in budgeted figures during periods with decreased or highly increased sales.

2. **Percentage-of-profit method.** This method is much like the previous one, except profit is used as the benchmark rather than sales. This method also has the same disadvantages.

3. **Objective-and-task method.** This method is probably the soundest budgeting method. Here the budgeter must specify exactly the role IMC has within the marketing plan and what the outcome of the IMC plan will be. Budgets are then based on this expected outcome. For example, the communications objective could be to increase regional sales for the top DMA by 6 percent over a three-month period. The following steps should be followed in generating budgeted amounts for the IMC variables.

   a. Specify the marketing objective to be achieved (profits, sales, market share, etc.).
   b. Specify the IMC mix variables that are needed in order to achieve this particular objective (i.e., advertising, public relations and publicity, and cybermarketing personal selling, sales promotion, direct marketing, advertising, and public relations and publicity).
   c. Specify the role of each of the IMC variables in achieving this expected outcome. In other words, is advertising needed? Sales promotion? Direct marketing?
   d. Specify the levels of measurable response in achieving these goals. These goals must be quantifiable and measurable.
   e. Budget dollar amounts based on the actual time needed to accomplish the desired IMC objectives.

4. **Competitive match or follow-the-leader method.** In this method, the IMC budgeter simply copies the IMC budget of the competition. The leader's budget may be matched, exceeded, or undercut. The basic idea of follow-the-leader is to assume that the industry leader is in the best position to calculate how much money should be expended on the IMC functions.

5. **All-you-can-afford method.** In this method, the budgeter looks at the funds that remain after all other budgets have been developed. Whatever is left over is spent on IMC.

6. **SWAG method.** This method is utilized either by budgeters who have little experience in budgeting or those who have a lot of experience in budgeting. It is simi-

lar to the all-you-can-afford method in that it is a very subjective method of budgeting. The planner simply guesses what funds will be needed to achieve any given goals. This guess is based on past experience and on the spending history of the company.

In reality, most budgeters rely on all these methods to develop the most cost-effective and accurate budget possible. Also, the advertising firm often sets a budget amount with input from the advertising agency or IMC planner. It is then up to the IMC manager to decide in which areas these dollars need to be spent. As the manager moves toward specific IMC mix variables, more microbudgeting takes place. The IMC mix managers must also develop desired budgets for their particular areas, thus giving the IMC vice president or account executive a better idea of what is needed for each of the various areas.

IMC Strategy Development

Only after a thorough situational analysis has been made at both the marketing level and the IMC level can decisions about strategy begin. The strategy consists of an overall direction to be taken by the IMC mix manager to best achieve the desired objectives. The following elements should be considered when developing an overall strategy: IMC expenditures, message positioning, the targeting and execution of messages, and brand equity. The strategy should be consumer-focused yet provide a direction to all of those involved in the IMC function. Two approaches (or sometimes a combination of the two approaches) can be used to facilitate strategic development. The first approach involves the following steps:

1. Identify the main problem for which IMC can provide a solution.
2. Identify the creative strategy needed to solve the problem. Include consumer perceptions, competition, product benefits, and legal requirements.

The second approach is more detailed and includes the following steps:

1. Know your customers. What do they like? What are their psychographics? Demographics? Geographics? Behavioristics?
2. Does the product fit the group?
3. Understand your competitors.
4. List the competitive advantage.
5. List what makes the product benefit believable to the consumer.
6. Set specific IMC action objectives. Is direct versus indirect action required?
7. Be proactive. In other words, plan for tomorrow.

The IMC strategy section deals with the development of an overall IMC strategy. Note that each of the IMC mix variable areas will also develop a strategy for their function and that these strategies must be consistent with the overall IMC strategy. An outcome of strategic development should be that each of the following steps has been satisfied:

1. *Identify and specify the key fact.*   Why (or why not) are consumers purchasing the product? This key fact should be written from a consumer's point of view.
2. *Identify and specify the key marketing problem.*   This should be based upon all prior research and written from the IMC manager's point of view.
3. *Identify, specify, and list the key IMC objectives.*   In other words, what specifically is the desired outcome?
4. *Identify and specify the creative platform (or message strategy).*   The creative platform must contain the target market, the primary competition, reasons why to purchase, and a consumer promise (the answer to the consumer's problem or a major benefit of the product for the consumer).

5. ***Establish strategy essentials.*** Remind the strategist to include uncreative information, as well as creative information (e.g., tag lines, logos, slogans, and legal requirements). Remember that the overall IMC strategy will guide individual IMC mix variable strategies, which in turn will guide the tactical executions of the IMC campaign.

IMC Tactics

The IMC tactics are the executionable aspects of the campaign. They are usually developed by specific function managers, based on the marketing and IMC plans. Each tactical execution must be based on the overall IMC strategy. A failure to do this will result in a campaign that is not integrated and that sends mixed messages to the consumer. Thus advertising, personal selling, sales promotion, direct marketing, public relations and publicity and cybermarketing will each develop individual plans that include objectives, strategies, and tactical executions to allow the successful launch of an IMC campaign.

The IMC Plan

The IMC plan is simply the outcome of all IMC mix variable plans. The plan must be integrated by the IMC manager and presented to the head of marketing to make sure it has an integrated fit with the overall marketing program. In addition, the IMC plan must have resource allocations, including budgeting for dollar, capital, and human resources.

Evaluation Methods

The IMC plan must have a section on how the IMC campaign is to be evaluated. Because the IMC objectives are measurable and quantifiable, this evaluative procedure should refer back to the objectives and indicate how they were achieved. It is common practice to rely on outside research organizations to assist, or even carry out, this evaluative function. The cost of the evaluation procedure, and changes in the IMC plan based on these evaluations, should also be specified. The following techniques can be used as evaluative tools for campaigns:

1. ***Concept tests.*** These can be used to test strategy as well as outcomes. Concept tests are qualitative, so the data may not be generalizable to all situations. Concept testing can be done through in-depth interviews, focus groups, or one-on-one interviews.
2. ***Copy testing.*** This test can also be used as an exploratory tool to predict if copy is going to be effective or if it was, in fact, effective. The effectiveness for various geographic regions can be tested to see if any changes in copy are needed or warranted.
3. ***Tracking studies.*** These are used while the campaign is being executed. Usually outside research specialists utilize on-going consumer surveys to monitor sales (among other things). The basic variables that are studied include (a) awareness, (b) product satisfaction, (c) product usage, (d) consumer attitude, and (e) consumer message recall. Tracking study data come primarily from mall intercepts, diaries, scanner data, and telephone interviews. Nielsen is the largest provider of these types of data.
4. ***Posttesting.*** Posttesting occurs after IMC executions have been completed. It allows the marketer to see if objectives have been reached and to understand the aspects of the campaign that were effective and those that were not. The most popular methods for posttesting are (a) the recognition test, (b) sales effects, (c) recall, (d) attitudes, and (e) awareness and likeability.

It is important to realize that the advertiser or IMC executive is looking for something in return for his or her investment in IMC. This something generally turns out to be sales. Thus, the IMC researcher must be able to show the marketer or advertiser exactly what the campaign has accomplished or hopes to accomplish in sales, profits, communications, idea generation, and so on. Without a successful evaluation plan, the advertiser or marketer will not choose a particular agency or individual to handle the all-important function of IMC management and execution.

The following chapters are devoted to the development of tactical executions for the IMC mix variables. They deal with advertising, sales promotion, public relations and publicity, direct marketing, and personal selling in detail. But first, it is important to collect all of the planning information. Figure 2–5 allows the insertion of data and information that will be useful in the development and execution of the IMC campaign. Fill in the blanks, for the information will be used. Utilize all of the information from the marketing plan outline to help develop an individualized IMC plan.

FIGURE 2–5 An IMC Plan Template

IMC Mission and Vision Statement:

Mission:

Vision:

IMC Situational Analysis: Include all relevant information, including product history, competitive analysis, geographics, psychographics, and behavioristics. Also be sure to include the IMC targeted market.

Company analysis (where we are now and how we got here):

Product/Service History/Analysis:

Competitive and Industrial Analysis/Evaluation:

    Competition:

Industry data:

Geographics (market analysis):

Current users/consumers evaluation:

Target market:

Overall IMC Objectives:

Budget (Include Budgeting Method):

IMC Strategy:

Evaluation Methods:

CHAPTER

Advertising

Just as there is no one perfect IMC plan, there is also no one perfect advertising plan. Every situation that requires advertising may have a different method for obtaining results. Advertising may be the key element of the IMC plan. For companies that are heavily involved with consumer products, this is certainly the case. For companies that are more active in business-to-business sales, advertising probably plays a smaller role than personal selling. No matter which situation one is involved in, advertising needs to be effective.

So what makes advertising effective? From the advertiser's point of view, advertising is effective if it generates sales and, thus, profits. From the IMC manager's point of view, advertising is effective if it achieves the goals or objectives stated in the IMC and the marketing plan. The truth is, advertising's effectiveness changes from situation to situation. It depends on timing and the general environment, which has an impact on the advertising. As stated earlier, the *only constant in the universe is change;* thus advertising has to be dynamic and flexible. The following are considerations that the advertising planner should take into account when developing effective advertising.

- ***Advertising must be dynamic.*** That is, it needs to be flexible.
- ***Advertising should be developed from a strategic point of view.*** It should follow the strategies developed in the IMC and marketing plans.
- ***Effective advertising is developed by keeping the consumer's needs paramount.*** The question should not be, What does the marketer or advertiser want? but rather, What does the consumer want?
- ***Advertising should be creative.*** It should be noted, however, that the creative elements of the advertising plan should not overshadow the strategies developed in the IMC and marketing plans.
- ***Effective advertising must be integrated.*** Advertising cannot make claims that are inconsistent with those strategies and objectives set for all elements of the IMC mix. Each mix variable must be consistent throughout the campaign. In addition, the advertising must not make promises that are not going to be delivered by the IMC execution. You can't promise someone excellent customer service while at the same time reducing service levels in the organization.
- ***Effective advertising must be persuasive and/or informative.*** The consumers must be given enough information to make a sound decision in terms of their needs.

The advertising plan is a carefully thought-out process used to guide the marketers in their attempt to sell products and services. As is the case with the marketing or IMC plan, a series of steps is taken in the development of an advertising plan. The steps are necessary to ensure that the advertising variable is integrated and that it is doing what it is supposed to in the overall scheme of things, that is, selling ideas, products, or services. In addition, the whole advertising plan must be integrated to allow for its successful completion. Some of the elements of the advertising plan may look redundant or repetitious, but it's important to note that many individuals will be working on the advertising at the same time and that they all need a common direction or goal; thus some repetition may be necessary. The outline in Figure 3–1 gives one method of advertising planning.

RESTATE THE TARGET MARKET

To aim the advertising plan at the consumer, the consumer must remain at the top of the advertiser's mind. All advertising should be directed toward those individuals who will actually use the product. Instead of guessing, the research that was undertaken to identify the target market should be utilized. Generally, the target market is defined in terms of the four "ics" discussed in chapter 2 (geograph*ics,* psychograph*ics,* demograph*ics,* and behaviorist*ics*). The advertising planner may want to increase this section by adding individuals who fit the various categories developed in the consumer evaluation portion of the IMC plan. In other words, how many of the consumers live in the East? West? North? How many are heavy users? Light users? Nonusers? How many are current users? Past users? Potential users? The advertising planner should try to visualize the targeted market to make it more real, or as one former executive at Hal Riney & Partners put it, to make them "real people." In addition to the statement of target audience, the advertiser may, and the advertising planner should, want to know the reason this particular market was chosen. In other words, explain why you've chosen this particular group of consumers to target. Provide rationale and support for your recommendations.

DEVELOP AND STATE THE ADVERTISING COMMUNICATION OBJECTIVES

Specifically, what effect is the advertising portion of the IMC plan going to have on the targeted market? This section should answer the question "What is the advertising supposed to do?" A programmed approach to setting objectives usually helps the advertising planner sell ideas to the management or advertiser in an easy-to-understand manner. Remember that the advertising objectives should flow from the overall marketing objectives, as well as the IMC objectives. There must be integration of all of the IMC areas to make the overall program effective. The following steps are recommended for the development of the advertising communication objectives.

- *Specify and state the key fact.* The key fact is a simple statement that gives all the information about such things as the product, environment, competitors, and target market—in other words, the most important aspect of the advertising plan. This key fact must be written from the consumers' perspective. It should indicate why consumers purchase the product and/or why they don't purchase the product. The key fact should be no longer than a paragraph, written in consumer language. It will serve as a guide for the development of the rest of the advertising plan, so it must be understandable.
- *Define the key marketing problem.* Based on the *key fact,* decide where advertising can have the most influence. The key marketing problem could stem from

1. Restate the target market.
2. Develop and state the advertising communications objectives.
3. Develop and state the advertising strategies (in particular the creative strategy).
4. Include creative execution samples.
5. List the media recommendations.
   a. Key problem
   b. Media objectives
   c. Media strategy
   d. Media plan

FIGURE 3–1 A Sample Advertising Plan Outline

any of the elements of the marketing plan. For example, it could be a product image problem or a product awareness problem. Perhaps it's a problem of product innovation or channels of distribution. It may be a pricing-related problem or a marketing communications problem. The key marketing problem should be short (usually less than half a page) and must be related to a situation in which advertising can have some type of impact. If advertising cannot solve the problem, or at least address the problem, it would be best left to some other area of integrated marketing communications or to the marketing department itself.

- *List the communications objectives.*   List the specific impact or effect that the advertising program is supposed to have on the consumer. What message is the advertiser trying to convey to the targeted market? How should the consumers react after being exposed to the advertising? This section should be limited to a couple of paragraphs. It works best if the objectives are "bulleted" and easy to read and understand.

The advertising planner must be sure that the objectives are written in an operational way. They should adhere to a set of criteria designed to facilitate understanding and provide communication. Objectives are used for evaluation purposes of advertising, so they must be clear. Always communicate the advertising objectives—short-term, intermediate, and long-term goals—in writing to all those individuals involved in the advertising planning process. It may also help to involve those people who will be undertaking the various processes of advertising to help achieve the objectives. Objectives are difficult to write and, because they provide direction for the overall campaign, must be clear and achievable. The following list may help in the development of well-written objective statements.

1. **Achievable and realistic.** The objectives must be attainable. Sometimes the advertising managers set objectives or goals that they would *like* to achieve but that cannot possibly be achieved by advertising alone. This is a bad situation, which could possibly create low morale in the work force, as well as have an impact on objective- and task-budgeting methods. Keep the objectives realistic and achievable.

2. **Measurable.** Because the objectives can (and probably will) be used as a measurement and evaluation tool, they must be quantified.

3. **Specific.** All objectives need to be specific in nature. They must explain exactly what should be achieved.

4. **Including time periods.** Generally an advertising campaign is set for a specific period of time (usually one year, although that isn't always the case). Objectives should reflect the progression of the campaign over a period of time. The planner may want to front-load the campaign to create awareness early on and then utilize frequency during the later portions of the campaign period. Setting time goals allows the campaign planner to evaluate the effectiveness of a campaign over the set period of time. This will allow for adjustments to the advertising and IMC mixes, generating more successful campaigns.

5. **Singular.** Each objective must be worded to allow for a specific outcome. Each objective should be associated with one, and only one, outcome. A one-outcome objective can be measured; perhaps even more valuable is the fact that each of the objectives becomes clear and provides guidance to the advertising manager.

6. **Cost effective.** Some type of cost-benefit analysis should be undertaken to see if the objective is worth the cost. Some objectives may be too expensive to undertake. If the campaign is limited by money (which most usually are), decisions have to be made about which objectives will generate the most value for the cost.

When writing the objectives it is important to remember that there is a desired outcome from each one. The writers should keep in mind which communication effect they are trying to achieve. Common objectives include the words *awareness, trust, attitude, image,* or *understanding.* When using these words as objectives, the writer must be sure that the desired direction of change is indicated in the objective. For example, the advertiser may want to set an objective dealing with product image. The objective must state exactly what direction this change should take. Does one want to increase a positive image? Reinforce a corporate or product image? Decrease awareness of the product image? Establish a specific image?

The development and writing of objectives is a difficult undertaking. It requires learned skills and a thorough understanding of the entire marketing and advertising plan. In addition, many professional advertising executives write faulty objectives. Remember, objectives can be changed. This change must emanate from an evaluation of the effectiveness of the campaign and an understanding of the marketing and advertising environments. Just because an objective wasn't achieved does not mean that it was a bad objective.

After a thorough review of the marketing and advertising plans, the advertising planner is ready to develop a strategy that will achieve the stated objectives.

ADVERTISING STRATEGY

The main idea of the advertising strategy is to develop and state the *creative message strategy,* or simply, the *creative strategy.* The creative strategy is also called the creative platform (and sometimes the copy platform). Up to this point our main concern has focused on planning the campaign. The creative strategy deals with what the advertising campaign will be communicating, that is, the message that is going to be communicated to the targeted audience or market. For the most part, the creative strategy is the most important aspect of the advertising campaign and thus is generally detail-oriented. A number of steps are involved in the development of an advertising strategy, and the campaign planner can use the following list as a guide.

- *Describe the target market (TM).* Instead of a paper definition, create a face for the targeted consumers. Use one or two sentences or statements that best describe the target market. Utilize the four "ics," as well as buying and media patterns (if appropriate), to give the targeted market a face. Make it real. For example, in Albuquerque, New Mexico, there is a new start-up manufacturer of high-tech running shoes. The company uses the name Z-Tech Footwear, Inc. After studying the market for high-tech running shoes, Z-Tech needs to develop a TM statement to be used for IMC in general and advertising in particular. Z-Tech's TM statement may read something like this:

> Z-Tech's target market consists of serious runners who have experienced a loss of energy or injury while running. The emphasis of the marketing should be placed on long-distance runners who have competed in long races, such as marathons, within the past two years. This market would include individuals in the United States who are between the ages of 18 and 45. These individuals enjoy running but find that there are injury problems and energy problems associated with the sport of long-distance running. In addition, because of future sales, Z-Tech thinks that the under 18- and over 45-year-old runners should not be ignored because they represent a significant source of potential income; therefore, these groups of runners will be defined as a secondary market.

Z-Tech, in the future, may wish to pursue other markets in the shoe industry but for now is concentrating on the core market of 18- to 45-year-old, serious, long-distance runners. This statement gives those involved in the execution of the advertising campaign a good general idea of where the advertising should be directed.

- *List the principle competition.* Not all competitors need to be listed, but certainly a short analysis of the major competition is warranted. Include the segment of the market in which the brand, service, or idea is competing. Within that segment, who are the key players? Based on this listing, what are the advantages and disadvantages of all of the competing brands? An understanding of the consumer's brand positioning within an intended market segment will help the advertisers position their particular brand or product. Be sure that the brand's advantages and disadvantages are also included in the analysis, not just the competition. This section should be limited to a paragraph. A chart or graph works very well here.

- *Provide a consumer promise.* What is the major selling idea? The planner needs to write (two-sentence maximum) a short promise to the consumer. Be sure the promise is written as a consumer benefit. This promise should provide a competitive advantage within the intended market segment. At times the promise can also be written as a solution to a consumer problem. The promise must generate strong consumer motivation, that is, make the consumer want to buy the product or service. In addition, the advertiser must make the promise believable to the consumer. Do not include advertising buzz words or jargon as part of the promise. Develop and write the promise in consumer language.

- *Give a reason why.* This statement is based on the consumer promise. It should be short (no longer than three sentences) and specific. Do not provide a list of product features; rather list the benefits that these features provide (again related to the consumer promise). The reason-why statement provides facts that support the consumer promise. Any factual information that will back up product claims should be included in this section. The facts should be relevant and informative, but more important, they should be interesting to the consumer. At times, certain consumer promises or claims are impossible to back up with scientific evidence; these are usually psychological or imagery types of claims. In these cases, an advertiser may want to turn to celebrity spokespeople or experts to support the claims being made by the product's advertiser. For example, Nike may want to use a popular athlete to endorse a product, thus alluding to the promise that if you wear the shoe, you'll perform better. On the other hand, Z-Tech uses a study undertaken by the Los Alamos Lab in New Mexico, to substantiate the fact that their shoes give more energy to the user.

- *Corporate or organizational requirements.* Corporate or organizational requirements must be included in the advertisements. For example, a company may require a specific tag line, or perhaps it feels that its logo must appear on any and all IMC activities. There may also be some legal requirements (e.g., for alcohol and cigarettes) that have to be included.

The advertising strategy provides the map for all other functions of advertising development. In addition, other members of the IMC team can utilize this strategy for the development of their tactical executions. It is recommended that all of this information be placed into a short but extensive layout. The following is a potential layout for an advertising strategy (also called copy platform).

SAMPLE COPY PLATFORM

Target audience:
Creative objective:
Advertising strategy:
1. Promise
2. Reason why
3. Product/brand/service consumer position
4. Corporate/organizational/legal requirements

Rationale:

- *Advertising rationale.* A rationale for all aspects of the strategy development must be provided. In other words, support and reinforce any and all recommendations in the advertising plan. This section allows for the defense of all ideas and concepts. Why were the objectives chosen? Why was this particular strategy chosen? In advertising there is no right or wrong, no black or white, only a best guess. List the reasons, with necessary support, for all recommendations. If a rationale isn't given for recommended advertising objectives and strategy, all of the work will probably be futile because people like to know how, why and where their investment is utilized. Without this type of information, the advertising recommendations are not worth the paper they're written on.

The following are some ideas for the generation of an advertising strategy. The table includes some of the main types of strategies used by advertisers.

Strategy	Description
Affective strategy	This strategy relies on consumer emotion to influence consumers. Humor is often utilized.
Brand imaging	This strategy attempts to create an image for the product or brand based on psychological claims.
Unique selling proposition	This strategy emphasizes a physical feature of the product or service that is better than that of the competition. If this strategy is utilized, there should be some proof of superiority.
Resonance strategy	This strategy is aimed at utilizing customers' experiences in trying to establish the product or brand as the one to buy. "Show and tell" works well with this type of strategy.
Product/brand positioning	This strategy is long term in nature and allows the advertiser to develop a unique position in the consumer's mind in relation to the competitors. Consumers tend to rank products according to some preconceived notion such as quality, price, or longevity.
Generic strategy	This strategy is used in a new market or in a market where a monopoly exists. This strategy simply provides a straightforward product benefit claim. There is no claim of superiority over the competition because it doesn't need it (either because there is no competition or the advertiser has a considerable market share and dominates the product category).

CREATIVE EXECUTIONS

At this point it is important to include a sample of tactical or creative executions that will help to show how the overall advertising strategy has been achieved. Include as many executions as are needed to provide the reader with the "big idea" for the campaign. Some of the creative executions that may be effective in achieving this important goal are listed here (this list is a sample and does not include all creative executions that may be important to the reader).

1. Print layout
2. Copy
3. Radio scripts
4. Storyboards
5. Out-of-home dummies

Before moving on to the development of the media portion of the advertising plan, an understanding of the advertising plan as a whole should first be demonstrated.

Figure 3–2 is an outline of the information required for successful completion of the first part of the advertising plan. Fill in the blanks. Once you understand the overall advertising function, move on to media development and recommendations.

MEDIA RECOMMENDATIONS

In this section of the plan, the advertiser lays out the media to be utilized during the advertising campaign. The media plan must be exhaustive, yet at the same time, as brief as possible. For new campaigns, the media plan will need to be fairly detailed. If this is an update or only a small change in the use of media from a previous plan, this section can be reduced significantly. However, some elements must be included. The key media problem must be addressed, as well as the media objectives, strategy, and plan. There should always be a rationale for all media chosen as part of the overall media plan.

The Key Media Problem

The key media problem deals with those situations that are solved by your unique media plan—that is, the vehicles you can use to get your message across to the targeted market. Set up the media problem to ensure acceptance from management for the advertising plan. For example, a key media problem may be changing a marketing plan to include support for the national sales force. The media must reach the national sales force, as well as the targeted market, thereby changing the traditional, as well as business-to-business, media.

Media Objectives

Just as in the other areas of the IMC mix, the media objectives must be realistic and quantifiable. The client will want to know that the objectives set for the media are being met. This section must be integrated with all the areas of marketing, as well of those in the integrated marketing mix. Generally, media objectives use a unique language; thus the media planner (as well as all those involved in the IMC plan) must be aware of and understand the terms used in setting media objectives. Remember, the overall goal of setting media objectives is to make sure that marketing strategies and objectives are translated into objectives that can be met by the use of media. The following areas (at least) should be addressed when developing the media objectives:

1. Reach and frequency
2. Continuity
3. Geographic or market weighting
4. Budget constraints and availability
5. Targeted market and audience
6. Gross rating points (grps)
7. Length of campaign
8. Integration with other areas of the IMC mix (i.e., personal selling, sales promotion, direct marketing, and public relations and publicity)
9. Flexibility

Include, also, a rationale for each of the media objective decisions made.

FIGURE 3–2 A Template for an Advertising Plan

Target Market:

Advertising Communication Objectives:

Key fact:

Key marketing problem:

Advertising communications objectives:

Advertising Strategy:

    Describing the target market:

    Principle competition:

    Consumer promise:

    Reason why:

    Corporate/organizational requirements:

Sample Copy Platform (if desired):

Rationale:

Sample Creative Executions (if desired):

THE 5 W'S OF MEDIA PLANNING

The *5 W's* associated with media planning are who, when, why, what, and where. Each must be addressed somewhere in the media plan. The *who* refers to the targeted market and audience, the *when* is associated with the timing of the overall media selection (media scheduling), the *why* provides a rationale for each of the various media decisions, and the *what* indicates what should be communicated in the various media and *where* the amount of resources (usually budgeted cash) should be allocated to the various media.

THOSE PESKY MEDIA TERMS

Appendix D provides a brief explanation of some of the terms used by media planners. The most utilized terms are explained here.

Reach

Reach refers to the percentage of the targeted audience that is exposed to a particular method, at least one time during the campaign's time frame. This percentage and the corresponding time frame are generally for four weeks. Everyone that is exposed to the message (at least once) during that four-week period is said to have been *reached*. The audience may have been reached more than once, but this should not be considered in calculating overall reach. Also, media planners use the terms *unduplicated reach, cumulative audience* (referred to as a *cume*), and *net coverage*. These terms are addressed in appendix D. As a rule, more people are reached by using multiple media vehicles, so the same campaign may appear in *Reader's Digest, Playboy, Cosmopolitan* and *TV Guide,* as well as appearing on *Frasier, Seinfeld,* and *Beverly Hills 90210.* For certain messages, media planners may try to extend reach by utilizing outdoor media (or outdoor plant), the radio, and perhaps newspapers. When setting a reach objective, remember that the more people reached, the higher the cost of advertising. Reach is not the only objective utilized by media planners. Reach only tells how many people (in percentage form) were exposed to a given message. It does not tell the media planner how many times these people were exposed. To indicate the exposure rate for the number of times the audience was exposed to the message, media planners use the term *frequency*.

Frequency

Frequency refers to the average number of times (during a given period, generally four weeks) the target audience is exposed to the advertiser's message. Frequency is also referred to as *average frequency* because the number used to estimate frequency is, in reality, an average. For example, let's assume that 80 percent of the targeted audience is *reached* at least one time. Let's say that out of that 80 percent, 30 percent are reached two times, 20 percent are reached three times, 20 percent are reached four times, and 10 percent are reached five times. The frequency would be 3.125.

$$\frac{(30 \times 2) + (20 \times 3) + (20 \times 4) + (10 \times 5)}{80} = \frac{250}{80} = 3.125$$

Gross Rating Points (GRPs)

Thus, in this example, 80 percent of the market is *reached* with a frequency of 3.125 during the four-week scheduling period. Gross rating points (GRPs) are the weight given to a particular advertising schedule. The GRP figure shows the media planner how much weight is required to generate sufficient reach and frequency to meet the media objectives. The GRPs indicate the *duplicated audience,* or *gross coverage,* for a particular media schedule. Remember, *reach* refers to unduplicated coverage (referred to as *unduplicated audience* or simple *net coverage*). To calculate the GRP, the media planner has to multiply reach times frequency.

$$\text{GRPs} = \text{reach } (r) \times \text{frequency } (f)$$

For the previous example, the reach was 80 and the frequency was 3.125, giving the media planner 250 GRPs.

$$80 \times 3.125 = 250$$

The media planner must then decide how many GRPs are needed to deliver the required amount of reach and frequency. Because the media schedule is developed before the reach and frequency have been obtained, ratings are used as indicators of the reach. *Ratings* are percentages of the population exposed to a single issue or broadcast of a particular medium (television, radio, newspaper, magazine, etc.). Some companies monitor ratings for any given medium; for example, Nielsen provides ratings (or reach) for television, and Arbitron provides similar information for radio.

Continuity

Another important media objective is *continuity*. To create continuity, the media planner must address the timing of the advertising campaign, that is, how advertising is allocated over the entire IMC or advertising campaign. The major decision is when the advertising should run. Many choices are available. For example, planners may want the advertising to run throughout the entire IMC campaign, or they may opt to front-load the campaign by spending a lot of money early in the time period and then reducing the amount spent over the rest of the campaign. In any case, the issue of when to schedule is determined by the personal thoughts of the media planner and marketers, as well as the type of product or service being advertised. Think of a political campaign and decide when is the best time to advertise, given a budget constraint. Keep in mind that a uniform campaign may not offer enough weight during important periods, whereas a concentrated or loaded campaign may leave you with no advertising during certain periods. For the most part, three choices are available to the media planner when determining the continuity of the campaign: continuous, pulsing, and flighting.

Continuous Scheduling

Continuous scheduling provides for equal amounts of advertising expenditures throughout the advertising campaign. This schedule assumes that consumption of the product or service occurs evenly throughout the year (or campaign period). If consumption or usage is not continuous—in other words, if there are high periods of consumption—perhaps continuous scheduling is not the best method to use to create continuity.

Pulsing

In pulsing, some advertising is used continuously throughout the campaign period; however, as opposed to the continuous schedule, the amount of the advertising expenditure is changed. Thus, if one is selling toys, they may be advertised throughout the year but with special emphasis (in dollar amounts) during the high consumption periods, probably October through December.

Flighting

In flighting, there may be no advertising expenditures in certain months but large expenditures in others. Thus the toy manufacturer may wish to allocate all of the advertising dollars during the months of October, November, and December, with no allocation during the other months. There is some similarity between pulsing and flighting; however, with pulsing, each time period during the campaign will use *some* advertising dollars, but in flighting there may not be any dollar amount for the period.

Cost Per Thousand (CPM)

The last step in setting media objectives must deal with the associated costs of advertising. In an attempt to allocate funds in the most cost-efficient manner possible, the media planner must utilize CPMs (cost per thousand). The *CPM* refers to the cost of reaching 1,000 people. Generally, the advertiser wants to calculate the costs associated with reaching 1,000 people in the targeted audience, so the CPM is representative of that market. The media planner must be careful about which audience the CPM is being calculated for. There can be a major difference in CPMs in general and CPMs for a given targeted audience. To be sure that everyone is talking about the same costs, the CPM for the target market (or audience) is often referred to as the CPM-TM (cost per thousand for the target market). The calculation for a CPM is quite easy. The cost of the ad is divided by the number of its total contacts (or for CPM-TM, the number of its total targeted market contacts).

$$CPM = \frac{\text{Cost of the advertisement}}{\text{Number of contacts (in thousands)}}$$

$$CPM = \frac{\text{Cost of the advertisement}}{\text{Number of targeted contacts (in thousands)}}$$

The media planner must be careful not to misuse the cost-per-thousand data by relying too heavily on the numbers. The CPM data do not necessarily work when dealing with different media, which provide different avenues for the media planner. Thus a radio CPM may be lower than one for television, but television may provide a function that radio simply cannot, that of show and tell. Even in the same medium, the media planner must be careful not to unwisely compare CPMs. For example, it may not be appropriate to compare the CPM of drive time versus morning time on a radio station or the costs associated with two- versus four-color advertising in a print medium. The advertiser may be looking for impact or for the ability to provide the product or service in the best manner possible.

It is important to note that many other terms associated with media planning can be found in appendix D.

When developing the media objectives, the planner must realize that each of the objectives of cost, reach, frequency, GRPs (or weight), and continuity have an adverse relationship with one another. That is, to generate greater reach, some frequency may have to be sacrificed, and vice versa. Given a fixed budget, the media planner must decide which of the objectives are the most important. Certainly, greater continuity can be achieved, but what is the impact and sacrifice from a CPM point of view? What is the impact on the frequency during important time periods? The media planner must take into account all aspects of the product or service. Is it a new product? If it is, frequency may be more important. Has the brand reached maturity in the product's life cycle, and is it well known? If this is the case, reach may be more important. Each media specialist needs to take into account and integrate all aspects of the marketing plan and IMC program before making decisions that could destroy a brand or elevate it to new sales heights.

MEDIA STRATEGIES AND RATIONALE

The media strategies provide actions for the media plan, and a rationale must be provided for each of the selected media. Thus, in the media strategy section, each of the media selected is listed and support for each of the media recommendations is provided as a rationale. The overall purpose of the media strategy is to offer guidelines that will translate the media objectives into a plan that guides the media planner's selection and use of the various media. Each of the media strategies selected must relate back to each of the media objectives. This may require the media manager to explain why certain strategies were not used. In addition, if nontraditional media are being used, there should be some explanation of why they are more effective. The following list provides information that should be addressed in developing effective media strategies. This list is not inclusive but is given as a general guideline.

- Types of media selected (i.e., the media classes)
- Allocation of the budget to the various media classes, including dollar amounts and the percentages of the total budget
- Budget allocation strategy for the various geographic regions (national, regional, national roll-out, spot only, etc.)
- Time-period budget allocation (monthly, yearly, quarterly, etc.)
- Reach and frequency levels desired
- Market sizes (primary, secondary, etc.)
- Market weighting
- CPM
- Media units to be used (30- or 60-second advertisements; full page, quarter page, half page print ads; etc.)
- Media schedule
- Key competitor analysis and strategy relationships
- Criteria utilized to select media
- Criteria utilized to schedule media
- Rationale for each of the strategic decisions

Since the media strategies should deal with how the media objectives will be fulfilled, they should be expressed in a series of statements. These statements can then be measured against the results of the campaign to see if, in fact, they were successful. The monetary allocation function of the media strategy becomes important at this point. Numerous IMC managers have chosen to allocate the budgeted funds according to seasonality, geographic markets with the greatest sales, and target audiences that have proven to be good customers (heavy users of a product, brand-loyal users, etc.). To summarize, the strategic elements of the media plan could fall under the following basic areas: (1) media mix (and types of media), (2) media classes (and formats), (3) media geographics, (4) media seasonality, and (5) flighting versus continuity.

The Media Mix   This strategic decision is based on the need for a mix of media (or no mix). If a mix is used, this strategy should indicate which media these will be. A strategic statement here could be this: "We will use only television as our advertising medium." Appendix E gives the advantages and disadvantages of the various media available to the media planner. Decisions can be based, in part, on the various media advantages. However, the media planner should be as creative as possible when developing media to use for the advertising plan. A disadvantage of one medium may be outweighed by its advantages, so use the appendix as a guide rather than gospel.

Media Classes   If a mix of media is used, each of the subgroups of each medium should be identified. For example, will spot or national network television be utilized? Which types of periodicals will be needed? An example of this type of strategy may be this: "We will only use Rodale Press monthly health magazines."

Media Geographics   What specific markets will receive the advertising? Methodologies utilized to identify specific markets must be included, as should information and methodologies used to exclude specific geographic markets. Many advertisers refer to BDIs and CDIs to help make a good, research-founded strategic decision. An example of a media geographic strategy statement is this: "We will utilize the CDI as a starting point to identify which categories are strongest in which geographic regions. Based on the CDI, advertising dollars will be allocated to support this decision."

Media Seasonality   As in the geographic strategy statements, there has to be some research-based reason for selecting seasonality. The decision may be made to increase advertising in slower sales months to utilize idle plant capacity for production (although this isn't normally the case). The strategy may read, "To increase the use of idle capacity and to increase sales volume during the slow sales months for our beverage."

Flighting Versus Continuity   All of the strategy statements that deal with the flighting versus continuity issues of media planning must be consistent with the other strategic statements. There must be a statement of how the media plan will achieve the media objectives, which in turn will show how the IMC strategies will be achieved, which in turn will show how the overall marketing strategies and objectives will be met. So the strategy might be this: "To utilize a pulsing pattern throughout the campaign period, which allows for front-end loading to launch the new product during the roll-out phase of the campaign. . . ."

The Media Plan (or Tactics)

Finally the entire media decision-making process is brought together in what is known as the media plan or the media tactics. Generally, this portion of the media plan gives specific information about how the entire plan will come together and work. It also provides graphic information about what the plan will look like, usually in a series of flowcharts and graphs and/or tables. A number of items need to be included in this section, the following at a minimum to allow the decision maker access to all information (at a glance):

- Media vehicles
- Reach, frequency, and GRP (for the entire plan, as well as for quarters in the overall plan)
- Cost
- Flowcharts (for each market in which a separate media plan is needed), giving the media used, when the ads will appear (a time line), advertisement sizes, day parts (if needed), and GRP levels, as well as seasonality, planned budget expenditures, and reach and frequency levels
- Optional information, such as sales-to-advertising comparisons, user analyses, and reviews of the competitive sales and media use

Any graphs and charts that will allow the reader (and the advertiser) to quickly make decisions about the media should be included. Use your imagination to develop innovative and creative ways to display this type of information. If additional information is required, include it. If some information can be excluded, do so. These are just guidelines to help with the flowchart development. The following flowcharts show what a completed media plan may look like (Figures 3–3 to 3–6).

Rationale

Finally the defense of the entire media plan boils down to the rationale used to develop the media strategies. This part of the plan is where the reasoning for the media strategy decisions is provided, in other words, why the specific media strategies were chosen. The reader or advertiser needs a reason to "buy off" on the overall advertising or media strategy. Sometimes the rationale portion is quite long and extensive; however, at other times the rationale may be fairly obvious, so this section may be only one or two paragraphs. The media planner may want to provide supporting documentation from MRI or Simmons that helps to justify the decisions being made. The basic idea is to provide enough information to allow decision makers to understand the reasoning behind the media strategies that were selected. Before proceeding to the next chapter on sales promotions, fill in Figure 3–7. Include the key media problem, the media objectives, media strategies, and rationale. It is also a good idea to practice developing media flowcharts and schedules, which can appear in the media tactics section (the media plan).

There should be a thorough review of the information provided for advertising and media. There should be no mistakes, and any changes required should be made before the introduction of the advertising plan. Also, the plan must be reviewed to be sure that it is thoroughly integrated into the overall marketing program and the other variables associated with the IMC mix. Chapter 4 details the process used to develop and create the sales promotions portion of the IMC plan.

FIGURE 3–3 Perrier CY 1987 Media Plan

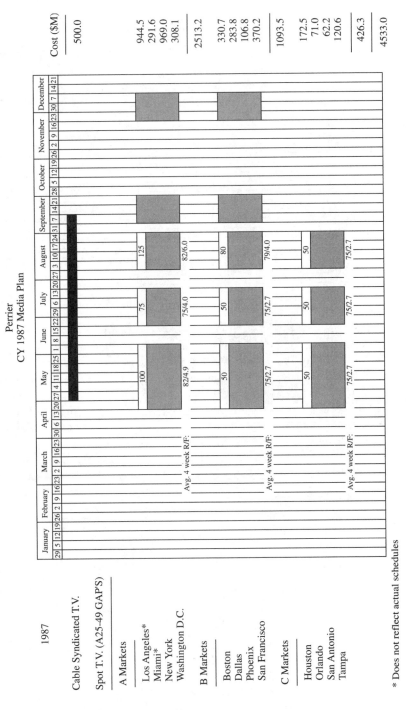

Perrier
CY 1987 Media Plan

*Does not reflect actual schedules

FIGURE 3–4 Perrier Approved 1988 Media Plan Magazine Schedule

Perrier
Approved 1988 Media Plan
Magazine Schedule

1988	January	February	March	April	May	June	July	August	September	October	November	December	$M
	4 11 10 25	1 8 15 22 29	7 14 21 28	4 11 18 25	2 9 16 23 30	6 13 20 27	4 11 18 25	1 8 15 22 29	5 12 19 26	3 10 17 24 31	7 14 21 28	5 12 19	
American Health	3X												72.9
Bon Appetit	4X												168.8
Food & Wine	4X												103.5
Gourmet	4X												140.2
GQ	4X												136.3
Metropolitan Home	4X												144.5
New Yorker	6X												179.3
People	6X												483.2
Travel & Leisure	4X												173.1
Traveler	4X												133.5
Vanity Fair	4X												155.2
Total	47X												$1890.5

■ = Spread 4CB
▨ = Page 4CB

Cumulative Reach/Frequency

Perrier Drinkers:	65/5.2
A25-49	53/4.4

4/12/88
CY88MAG

© 1988, 1988 Media Plan, Inc. Used with permission of Hal Riney & Partners, San Francisco, CA.

FIGURE 3–5 Calistoga CY 1987 Actual Media Plan

Calistoga
CY 1987 Actual Media Plan

1987	January	February	March	April	May	June	July	August	September	October	November	December	Cost ($M)
Spot Radio (60's) A18-34 GAPs													
Northern California													
San Francisco	Avg. 4 week R/F:			150 / 72/8.3	100 / 55/7.3	100 / 55/7.3	100 / 55/7.3	155 / 74/8.9					338.3
San Jose, Sacramento Santa Rose				50	50	50	50						66.0
Fresno, Modesto, Chico, Stockton, Santa Cruz/ Monterey				35	35	35	35						30.5
					Avg. 4 week R/F: 24/4.2 / Avg. 4 week R/F: 19/3.7								435.8
Southern California													
Los Angeles	Avg. 4 week R/F:			150 / 72/8.3	100 / 55/7.3	100 / 55/7.3	100 / 55/7.3	155 / 74/8.9					449.1
L.A. Times													32.5
													481.6
Denver					90	90	90	90					51.7
					Avg. 4 week R/F: 50/5.4								

969.1
Actualized
Expenditures

1/29/88

© 1988, 1988 Media Plan, Inc. Used with permission of Hal Riney & Partners, San Francisco, CA.

81

FIGURE 3–6 Perrier Approved 1988 Media Plan

Perrier
Approved 1988 Media Plan

1988	January	February	March	April	May	June	July	August	September	October	November	December	Cost ($M)	%
	20 4 11 10 25	1 8 15 22 29	1 7 14 21 28	4 11 18 25	2 9 16 23 30	6 13 20 27	4 11 18 25	1 8 15 22 29	5 12 19 26	3 10 17 24 31	7 14 21 28	5 12 19		
National Media														
Magazines - 11 Titles 41 Insertions						13	13	10	11				1890.5	39
Cable T.V. ESPN, A&E, NTBS													222.7	4
													2113.2	44
Spot T.V.*														
Early Morning 100 TA GAP's						20	20	20		Spot TV			944.5	20
Primetime/Select Sports 400 TA GAP's						50	50	50		Los Angeles			347.7	7
										Miami			55.4	1
Late News 320 TA GAP's						40	40	40		Miami Hispanic			971.8	20
Late Fringe 160 TA GAP's						20	20	20		New York			367.4	8
Hispanic TV Miami 10 Spots/Week						10	10	10		Washington			2686.8	56
													$4800.0	100

*Los Angeles, Miami, New York, Washington

![] = 50% : 60's (Except L.A.)

A25-49 R/F	Intro	Avg. 4 Wk.	Cume
Spot TV	85/6.1	76/4.5 (36% 4+)	92/11.3
Magazine			53/4.4
Cable			15/2.7
Total National			60/4.6
Spot + National			97/13.6

4/12/88
CY88Plan

82

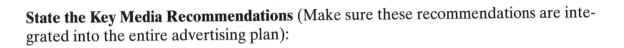

FIGURE 3–7 Media Recommendations

A Media Template

State the Key Media Recommendations (Make sure these recommendations are integrated into the entire advertising plan):

The key media problem:

Media objectives:

Media strategies:

Rationale:

Media Tactics: "The Media Plan" (Included here should be any flighting schedules, media flowcharts, or media schedules that will help the planners and advertisers understand the whole picture):

CHAPTER

Sales Promotion

As stated earlier, sales promotions are utilized to complement other elements of the IMC mix. Generally, sales promotions can be trade-related (such as sales force motivation) or consumer-related. Sales promotions must support the overall objectives of the IMC plan, as well as the marketing plan. They must be integrated into the overall objectives of the organization. In the past, sales promotions have been developed in conjunction with the advertising plan. It is suggested, however, that because of the complexity of today's IMC function, sales promotions should be treated as a separate category (keeping in mind that they must be integrated into the entire mix). Sales promotions have traditionally been used to generate a short-term increase in sales. However, these promotions, if properly planned, can also have an impact on long-term sales. Research has found that sales promotions for consumer goods are particularly successful during the maturity phase of the product's life cycle, as well as the introductory phase. Trade promotions are used to recruit or increase the numbers of channel-of-distribution members and to motivate them to pay special attention or provide more service to a particular brand or product.

TRADE PROMOTION

Trade promotions are aimed toward the intermediary members of the channel of distribution (i.e., the retailers and wholesalers). As stated earlier, sales promotions can provide a tangible reason to do something (like a bribe). Many types of sales promotions are used for the trade; the following list includes the major kinds:

1. Trade allowances
2. Cooperative advertising
3. Vendor support programs
4. Trade contests and incentives
5. Point of purchase (POP) materials
6. Training programs
7. Specialty advertising
8. Trade shows

To better understand the functions of these areas, it may help to look at each one individually.

TRADE ALLOWANCES

The objectives behind trade allowances are to increase purchases of manufacturers' brands and products by wholesalers and retailers, as well as to increase the consumers' purchases of the manufacturers' brands from the resellers. It should be noted here that many retailers pocket some of the trade allowance dollars (it has been estimated that this figure is around 30%) rather than passing them on to the consumer.

There are many different types of trade allowances, including (but not limited to) off-invoice, bill-back, slotting, exit fees, forward buying, diverting, everyday low pricing (EDLP), efficient consumer response (ECR), and pay-for-performance.

- *Off-invoice allowances* are deals offered periodically to the trade that permit wholesalers and retailers to deduct a fixed amount from the invoice. Manufacturers hope to increase retailers' purchases of their brands, thus increasing consumers' purchases of the brand, by passing on the savings to the consumers in the form of reduced prices.
- *Bill-back allowances* are given to retailers for featuring the manufacturer's brand in advertisements or for providing special displays. The retailer bills the manufacturer for services rendered, and the manufacturer pays an allowance to the retailer for the services received on behalf of the manufacturer's brand (or service).
- *Slotting allowances* are quite common, especially among food retailers. Slotting allowances are fees the manufacturer pays a retailer to carry the manufacturer's product or service. The term *slotting* refers to the shelf or display space of the retailer. Because of the cost associated with carrying a product (especially new products), the retailer wants a guarantee against losses. The slotting allowance is that guarantee. The problem arises with the value of a slot to a retailer versus a manufacturer. It is somewhat questionable whether the actual expenses incurred by the retailers are anywhere near the slotting allowances they charge. Some of these costs could include those associated with making space available in the distribution centers, creating new entries in the computer inventory systems, redesigning store shelves, notifying stores of the new product, or simply lost sales from an old product that was replaced by the new one.
- *Exit fees* are charges by retailers to remove a product from the shelf. The vendor, wholesaler, or manufacturer signs a contract with the retailer stipulating an average volume of weekly traffic during a specified period. If this volume is not achieved, the retailer charges the vendor for the removal of the product (also called a handling charge).
- *Forward buying and diverting* are also allowances. These trade allowances often induce retailers to purchase large quantities of products and then stockpile them in order to take advantage of a temporary price reduction. When the manufacturer restricts a deal to a limited geographic area, the wholesalers and retailers buy abnormally large quantities at the stated reduced price and then resell the excess quantities (generally through a broker) to wholesalers and retailers in other geographical areas. Large retailers can take advantage of forward buying by purchasing the brands with a trade allowance and then selling the product to customers at the regular price. Manufacturers' trade allowances are typically available every four weeks of the business quarter. During these periods, retailers buy larger quantities than they need and warehouse the excess inventory, thus avoiding the need to purchase the products at the full price. About one-fourth of all retail inventory is purchased through forward buying. Problems with forward buying for the IMC planner and marketer include the following:
  1. Only 30 percent of trade allowances to wholesalers and retailers is passed along to the customer; 5–10 percent of the products sold on trade allowances is diverted.
  2. Increased distribution costs are associated with forward buying and diversion. The retailer has to move the product from the warehouse to the store instead

of having the product on-hand for the consumer, thus creating a potential of lost sales.

3. Manufacturers receive reduced margins because of the price discounts they offer, as well as increased costs incurred for this process.

- To stop the dependence on forward buying and diversion, the *everyday low price (EDLP)* was developed. In this concept, first introduced by Proctor & Gamble in 1990, a manufacturer charges the same price for a certain brand, day in and day out. This solves the problems associated with forward buying and diverting because these trade allowances aren't offered to the retailers and wholesalers. The profit is made from selling the product, not from buying it. There is a lot of resistance to EDLP, and it is hard for some of the smaller companies to convert to a pure EDLP system. Three reasons for this resistance are the following:

1. Many retailers have already developed distribution infrastructures that avail themselves of high-low pricing. They have developed storage capabilities to take advantage of the manufacturers' deals. Thus the more committed the channel members are to forward buying, the more resistance they have to EDLP.
2. Some evidence exists that EDLP benefits the manufacturer more than the retailer, thus increasing resistance.
3. EDLP takes some of the excitement out of retail-level pricing. With EDLP the retailer always charges the same amount to the consumer. Without being able to offer attractive sales prices, retail pricing becomes monotonous, not only to the retailer, but also to the consumer. (Consumers haven't figured out that there is no benefit to the high-low pricing system and that they save money with EDLP.) This is extremely important to the IMC planner who is going to utilize an EDLP system for the product. In practice there is no pure EDLP.

- Generally EDLP is coupled with periodic promotional funding. *Efficient consumer response (ECR)* is a broad-based concept of business management that is oriented toward altering industry practices by the enhancement of efficiencies coupled with cost reductions. Numerous estimates indicate that each year approximately $30 billion is wasted because of inefficient ordering procedures and maintenance of excessive inventories. The objective of ECR is to improve efficiencies at all levels of the channel of distribution (wholesaler, retailer, and manufacturer) to reduce costs (especially to the consumer), as well as to reduce the huge expenditures for trade promotions.

- *Pay-for-performance programs* are a form of trade allowance designed to reward retailers for selling the brands so supported rather than merely buying them (by comparison, off-invoice allowances reward retailers for simply buying trade-supported brands). Pay-for-performance programs are also called scanner-verified trade promotions because the retail sales volume for a trade-supported brand is recorded by an optical scanning device. Pay-for-performance works like this: First, a manufacturer establishes, in conjunction with the retailer, a time frame in which the retailer receives an allowance for all quantities of the promoted brand that are actually sold to the consumer. A designated price is established. Second, the retailer's own scanning data verify the exact amount sold in the designated time frame. Third, after determining the scanned quantity, the manufacturer pays the retailer the designated difference on the quantity sold plus compensation for the amount of the trade allowance on that same quantity sold. Thus, the manufacturer is not paying for a trade allowance on items that are not sold. IRI and A.C. Nielsen are moving into the role of scanning agents, providing the scanning function for a number of businesses. *Cooperative advertising* is a trade promotion used to enable manufacturers to achieve advertising support in a local market, giving them ways to associate their products and brands (in the consumers' minds) with specific retail outlets. Reasons to use cooperative (co-op) advertising include:

- Consumers of infrequently purchased goods are more responsive to retailers' advertisements, especially preceding a major buying decision. Without the co-op dollars, the retailers would not emphasize the manufacturer's product in their advertisements.
- Retailers, knowing they have accrued co-op dollars, are more likely to aggressively promote that merchandise.
- Co-op advertising allows the manufacturers to have access to local media at an advertising rate lower than they would have to pay if they advertised directly, rather than through the retailer (local media have lower rates for local advertisers than for national advertisers).
- From the retailer's perspective, co-op advertising is relatively inexpensive for the amount of advertising received.

For planning purposes, five elements are common to all co-op advertising programs:

1. A specified time period
2. Accrual (the retailer receives an accrual account or advertising fund from the manufacturer, based on a fixed amount or percentage of a retailer's net purchases from the manufacturer during the specified term of the co-op contract)
3. Payment share (or participation rate), which is the amount the manufacturer reimburses the retailer for advertising
4. Performance guidelines (the manufacturer's requirements that the retailer must satisfy to qualify for reimbursement)
5. Billing for reimbursement (which basically just states what forms need to be submitted to get the reimbursement)

When planning for co-op spending, the IMC planner needs to include trade associations, which can influence the spending of co-op advertising dollars. The association will pool co-op dollars from the independent retailers who cannot afford the time to produce a monthly newspaper ad featuring the manufacturer's products. Trade associations can also present the legal aspects of co-op usage to small-business committees, as well as motivate smaller retailers by designing the insert with editorial copy and national ads, allowing a page for the local retailer to place co-op ads and store identification. They can also negotiate for the smaller retailers with the manufacturers.

Vendor support programs are designed to help the retailer. The retailer, in this situation, would have greater channel control than the manufacturer, who is competing for available shelf space. The retailer develops an advertising program in consultation with local advertising media and then invites its suppliers to pay for a specific percentage of the cost of the proposed campaign.

Trade contests and incentives are developed by manufacturers to encourage better performance from retail management personnel and sales staffs. A trade contest is typically directed at the store or department level and generally is based on meeting a sales goal that is established by the manufacturer. Whereas trade contests are typically related to sales goals, trade incentives are given to retail managers and their salespeople for the performance of specific tasks. One type of sales inventive is called "push money" (PM), also known as "spiffs." The manufacturer provides cash to salespeople to encourage them to push certain products in the manufacturer's line. The spiff should encourage salespeople to favor the manufacturer's models over those of competitors.

Point-of-purchase advertising, or materials, are items designed by the manufacturer's IMC planners to attract consumers' attention by enhancing the attractiveness of displayed merchandise and to assist the retailer in using store space more efficiently. It should expand product-category sales volume and/or increase store traffic.

Training programs are used to create more knowledgeable sales personnel. With increased knowledge comes greater confidence and more effort devoted to specific products and services. The investment in employee knowledge has become an important strategic function for IMC planners, especially with the shift to international marketing communication management.

Specialty advertising is used to complement the other forms of marketing communications by providing another way to keep the company's name, logo, tag line, and so forth before the customers and prospects. By definition, specialty advertising utilizes useful or decorative articles to transmit an organization's identification and/or promotional message to its targeted audience. There are two methods for specialty advertising: (1) random distribution (e.g., matchbooks, calendars, pens, pencils, business cards, T-shirts, and caps) and (2) structured promotion, which calls for the planning and analyzing of the promotional objectives, including target audiences, promotional themes, budgets, and distribution methods.

Specialty advertising can help to accomplish the following IMC objectives: the promotion of new store openings, the introduction of new products, the motivation of salespeople, the establishment of new accounts, the development of trade show traffic, improved customer relations, and the activation of inactive accounts.

Trade shows are a temporary forum for sellers of a product category to exhibit and demonstrate their wares to present and prospective consumers. It is estimated that over 1.3 million companies were active in trade shows throughout the United States and Canada last year. The specific functions of a trade show include the following:

1. Servicing customers
2. Identifying prospects
3. Introducing new and modified products and product lines
4. Gathering information about the competition
5. Taking product orders
6. Enhancing a company's image

When using trade shows as a form of promotion, the planner should develop a plan that provides for (1) products and services (what you want to offer the customer), (2) top prospects, (3) show analysis, (4) goals, (5) booth information, (6) typical work forms, and (7) staffing and training of trade show personnel.

Objectives   The major objectives of trade promotions are to persuade wholesalers to distribute a product and to persuade retailers to stock the product. To develop your own objectives, first start with a description of what the sales promotion function is supposed to achieve. Make the recommendations as specific as possible. Utilize objectives that have been written specifically for the marketing plan. Pay particular attention to the strategies being developed for the marketing plan, as well as the IMC plan.

Strategy   The strategies for trade promotions should be logical deductions from the rest of the IMC plan. The strategies should provide information on how the objectives set for trade promotions will be met. Again, the objectives indicate what needs to be accomplished, whereas the strategies tell how this will be done.

Tactics   Tactics for trade promotions indicate the specifics of the planned events for the trade promotions. Because there may be many events, there should be tactics for each one. Be sure to differentiate each of the various trade promotion tactics with the trade promotion strategies and events.

Rationale   You must provide reasons for the various trade promotion activities, that is, justify their undertaking. The rationale should be as quantitative as possible. State the rationale so that it shows long-term, as well as short-term, benefits to the manufacturer or advertiser. Also, there should be some coverage of how these promotional activities are integrated into consumer-oriented promotions and the IMC plan as a whole.

Evaluation   All promotion activities must be evaluated and controlled to assess which methods work best for your particular plan. Certainly some types of promotions are easier to evaluate than others, but there must be an indication of which evaluative techniques are going to be utilized to test the effectiveness of the promotions. The IMC planner can refer to the objectives of the trade promotions to find out if these have been achieved. If they haven't, there must be a reason. Once the reason is identified, adjustments should be made to the sales promotions to achieve greater efficiency. Don't use methods that are ineffective just because "everyone else does."

CONSUMER SALES PROMOTIONS

Consumer sales promotions are aimed toward the end user, or final consumer. Certainly an understanding of what has worked well for the company or advertiser in the past would be a starting point for the development of consumer sales promotions. Basically, consumer promotions are incentives provided by an advertiser or manufacturer to stimulate the sales of a brand, product, service, or idea. The tools utilized in consumer sales promotions are diverse and generally stimulate short-term changes in sales. The difference between advertising and consumer sales promotions is that advertising gives the consumer a reason to purchase a particular service or product, whereas sales promotions provide the consumer (or prospective consumer) with an incentive to purchase a given product or service. The following is a list (although not inclusive) of the main types of sales promotion activities:

- *Sampling.* This is used to deliver an actual or trial-sized product to the consumer.
- *Point-of-purchase coupons.* Coupons are provided for the consumers where the purchases are made.
- *Mail- and media-delivered coupons.* These types of coupons offer delayed rewards for the consumer. Either the coupons are mailed directly to the homes of consumers or consumers are reached via some type of medium. One example of a media-delivered coupon is a free-standing insert (FSI). The FSIs are provided to consumers through a variety of media, the Sunday newspaper being a very popular vehicle.
- *In-pack or on-pack coupons.* These coupons are provided to consumers directly on the packaging of the product. The consumer can tear them off and use them immediately to purchase the product or, in some instances, can use them on their next purchase.
- *Premiums.* Premiums are types of merchandise or services given to the consumer to induce purchases. The three most popular premiums are free-in-the-mail (consumers send in proofs of purchase to receive some type of merchandise), self-liquidating (allowing the consumer to mail in a specified number of proofs of purchase along with a specified amount of cash to cover the handling and shipping and perhaps cost of the premium), and in- or near-pack premiums (merchandise is available in or is attached to the product's package).
- *Price-off promotions.* Consumers are given a reduction in the suggested retail price of a product or service.

- *Bonus packs.* These are extra quantities of a product given to the consumer at the regular price.
- *Refunds and rebates.* These are cash discounts or reimbursements given to the consumer for making a purchase. Lee Iacocca, when he was chairman of the board at the Chrysler Corporation, made the rebate popular with the advertising tag line, "Get a car, get a check."
- *Contests and sweepstakes.* These are opportunities for the consumers to win or earn cash or prizes from the manufacturer or advertiser.
- *Overlay and tie-in promotions.* Overlays are the tactical execution of two or more sales promotions activities at the same time; tie-ins involve the simultaneous promotion of multiple brands in a single promotional activity.
- *Product warranties or guarantees.*
- *Point-of-purchase displays.*

The first step in the development of sales promotion recommendations is to state the sales promotion objectives.

Objectives The objectives must include a complete description of what is to be achieved by the consumer sales promotion function. Be specific when developing the overall objectives. They have to be as quantifiable as possible and always measurable. They also need to be achievable, while at the same time providing a goal that will benefit all those involved in the process. Finally, the objectives need to be integrated into each of the variables of the IMC mix and the overall marketing plan. Without this integration, the objectives become worthless. Following is a list of potential sales promotions goals. It is up to the IMC planner to quantify each of the objectives that is developed.

1. Maintenance of current customers
2. Trial stimulation
3. Repeat usage amount by current customers
4. Multiple purchases
5. More frequent purchasing
6. New product introductions
7. New packaging
8. Event tie-ins
9. Geographical stimulation
10. Seasonal exploitation
11. Trade-ups
12. New usage

After the IMC planner understands the role that sales promotions should play in the IMC plan, a strategy has to be developed to guide the tactical executions needed to achieve the objectives.

Consumer Sales Promotion Strategies The strategies provide the specifics of the consumer sales promotion plan. All specific sales promotions techniques chosen be utilized should be listed here (see previous list for examples). It may be a good idea to also explain why certain techniques weren't utilized, although they were considered.

Consumer Sales Promotion Executions This section should include examples of the chosen sales promotion activities. Although some form of art is generally used, it is possible to present only descriptions of the activities. The purpose of including examples is to show everyone exactly what is to be used in the sales promotions and how these promotions tie in with the other IMC mix variables. Some of the more common executions include the following:

- Trial packages
- Sample packages
- Drawings or illustrations of proposed premiums
- Examples of coupons
- Layouts of ads that are concerned with contests or sweepstakes
- Point-of-purchase advertising dummies
- Take-one pads

Be sure that the tactical executions are integrated into the entire marketing plan, as well as the IMC mix.

Rationale   A rationale for each of the specified sales promotion activities must be provided. There must be justification, generally accompanied by costs, for each specific activity, thereby defending the key elements of the sales promotion plan. Again, if the planner can show that the sales promotions will benefit the advertiser in the long run, as well as in the short run, the sales promotion activities will have a better chance of being accepted for the IMC plan. The costs associated with each of the specific sales promotion activities must also be justified. A short cost-benefit analysis is usually enough.

Evaluation   Once the sales promotion activities have been developed, there needs to be some plan for the evaluation of their effectiveness. The planner may want to recheck the objectives to know what the sales promotions were supposed to accomplish. If these goals aren't achieved, the advertisers and planners should evaluate why. Changes need to be made, as soon as possible, to increase the effectiveness of the sales promotions. If the sales promotions were supposed to increase new product awareness and usage by 8 percent, but there is only a 4 percent increase, the marketer must find out why the goal was not achieved. There may be some very good, uncontrollable reasons—the goals were set too high, the economy changed, new competitive products were introduced, the competition increased its sales promotion spending, and so on. However, there may be a problem with the current sales promotion plan that needs adjustment. Basically, what must be included in the evaluation section of the plan are the methods that are to be utilized to evaluate or measure the success of the consumer sales promotion recommendations.

INTEGRATING TRADE AND CONSUMER SALES PROMOTIONS

Once each specific sales promotion is selected for the trade and the end-user, or consumer, there needs to be an integration of the two plans. To do this, IMC planners generally opt for a sales promotion plan. This plan is usually in calendar form, much like that of a media schedule. There should be an overall summary of the costs associated with each of the promotional activities. Remember that all sales promotional activities have a cost, perhaps not up front but somewhere during the campaign. For example, the planner should not forget to include the costs of coupon redemption or premium fulfillment. It may also be a good idea to include projected responses from each of the promotional activities, such as the number of coupons redeemed or of premiums needed. If there are sweepstakes and contests, the costs associated with these activities must also be included (prizes, judging, and the like). Put the time line for the sales promotions on a graph or chart to allow for easy comparisons between the advertising and sales promotion plans and for a way to track the entire IMC campaign.

Fill out Figure 4–1 with all the information required for the successful development of the sales promotion recommendations. Remember to utilize graphs, tables, and charts to help simplify the information for the reader.

FIGURE 4–1 Sales Promotion Recommendations

A Sales Promotion Plan Template

Sales Promotion Recommendations:

Trade:

Objectives:

Strategies:

Tactics:

Rationale:

Evaluation:

Consumer promotions:

Objectives:

Strategies:

Tactics:

Rationale:

Evaluation:

Sales Promotion Schedules. Insert the overall sales promotion to be used for both the trade and consumer promotions. Remember to include time lines and costs for each of the sales promotion activities:

Overall Sales Promotions Effectiveness (Evaluative Criteria and Tools). Include all methods that will be used to evaluate and measure the effectiveness of the sales promotion executions and plan. It would be a good idea to include a short paragraph about what will be done if the objectives are not met:

CHAPTER

Direct Marketing 5

D irect marketing is becoming more and more popular with different types of companies. The idea is to establish a direct relationship with a targeted person to generate an *immediate* response. The Direct Marketing Association (the largest trade association for businesses interested in database marketing) defines direct marketing as "an interactive system of marketing which uses one or more advertising media to effect a measurable response and/or transaction at any location." Direct marketing doesn't involve an intermediary, another channel of distribution. Thus, the idea behind direct marketing is to solicit an order, a request for further information, or a visit to a place of business for the specific purpose of buying a product or service. Direct marketing must attempt to solicit and close the sale.

Several categories of direct marketing can be utilized for a tactical attack on the targeted market. **Direct response advertising, telemarketing,** and **direct selling** are the three major categories of direct marketing. Direct response advertising includes the use of direct mail, electronic media, and print media, although new methods are also being developed. In telemarketing, the telephone is used to solicit and close sales. Direct selling is generally a function of the sales department and will be covered in more detail in chapter 7.

OBJECTIVES AND STRATEGY

Direct marketing techniques are used to support a comprehensive IMC plan. The marketer must develop a series of objectives for direct marketing that will complement the overall IMC campaign. The idea of direct marketing is to create a buyer-seller relationship.

RELATIONSHIP

Because of this objective, this type of selling is often called relationship marketing. The following list provides the major objectives of a direct marketing campaign. They should be useful to you when you develop your own direct marketing objectives. Again, remember that the direct marketing objectives must be related to each of the IMC mix variables.

1. Retention of current customers
2. Inducement of product trial
3. Brand switching
4. Increased sales or usage volumes
5. Sales through direct response

1. Retention of Current Customers   It is much easier, and cheaper, to retain a current customer than to generate new customers. Direct marketing provides programs, such as the Book of the Month Club, that help to establish and maintain a relationship with each customer. These are known as *continuity programs* because they attempt to develop continuity with the customer base.

2. Inducement of Product Trial   Direct marketing allows the advertiser to generate a list of potential customers, via a database, who may have a need for a product. The advertiser, using direct marketing, can then send trial samples of the product or coupons for a free or discounted product to the customers on the list.

3. Brand Switching   If the IMC planner or direct marketer secures a list of current users of a competitive brand, some type of direct mail piece could be generated that shows the user how the advertiser's product is more effective. A sample could be included for a hands-on demonstration of how effective this product is.

4. Increased Sales or Usage Volumes   Newsletters, frequent flier programs, and other affinity programs can be developed to encourage additional use of a product. The more often one purchases, the more points one gets. This type of program is beneficial for the customer, as well as the business. It increases product usage in addition to sales for the brand.

5. Sales Through Direct Response   Direct marketers like to generate sales through direct response advertising. The telephone makes an ideal vehicle for a response, causing an increase in sales. Numerous media may be employed to generate leads for direct response sales, but most of the sales are made on the telephone.

Based on the set objectives, the marketer is ready to develop the strategic approach. Because the marketer is directing the promotions to specific customers, it is very important to also develop what the potential customers will experience and how they will receive the message. The message may take the form of radio commercials, kiosks, or direct mail pieces. These are the creatives elements or tactics that will be used. Before developing the creatives, the marketer must develop a strategy (a creative strategy) to ensure that there is integration throughout the program.

THE STRATEGY

Several important points need to be developed in building a strategy. The following list will provide you, the marketer, with a basis for strategy development.

- *The product.*   The IMC planner for direct marketing must have a knowledge of the product. What is it? What does it do? It is of extreme importance when developing the creatives for direct marketing that the designer knows the product in detail before he or she tries to describe it to the prospects.
- *Competitive products.*   How does the competition's product compare to yours? By knowing the competition, direct marketers can favorably compare their products with those of the competitor. The major benefits of your product over the competition provide a perfect example of something that can be utilized in developing IMC or direct marketing creatives.
- *The market.*   The nature of the market will determine which creative strategical approach should be developed. If the product is a high-ticket automobile, for example, the creatives will most likely have a more sophisticated look than those that would be used for a low-priced item such as ketchup.
- *The media.*   The media are very important because the strategist must know where the creatives will be communicated. There is a major difference in commu-

nicating through a direct mail piece and on direct response television. Most media offer different advantages and disadvantages that will produce differing levels of information.

- *The budget.*   The budget is very important because the strategist needs to know what resources are available for the creation of the direct marketing promotions. For example, if a product is expected to do very well and generate a large profit, more could be spent on bringing in highly acclaimed outside talent.
- *The objective.*   The marketing and IMC objectives must be known and understood by all of those involved in the direct marketing process. The question direct marketing strategists should ask themselves is, "What are we trying to do to meet the overall IMC and marketing goals?"
- *Creative implementation.*   How will this information be utilized? How will it be organized? What is the copy theme? How can we execute it visually?

THE MEDIA

Various media can be used to effectively communicate the direct marketing message to the consumer. The following are the major media utilized in direct marketing.

Direct Mail

Direct mail is a very popular method of direct marketing in which a promotional piece is sent to a current customer or prospect. Popular direct mail pieces include catalogs, single-product packages, magalogs and polypak sample packages.

Catalogs are booklets that contain many products, which are usually related. For example, a computer-supplies catalog would contain many different computer-related products. However, many store catalogs contain products from all of their departments (women's wear, men's wear, children's wear, jewelry, etc.).

Single-product packages contain information about one product or service. A single-product package often includes a color brochure and letter, describing the product, as well as an order card.

A magalog is a recent development in direct mail. It is much like a single-product package except for the layout. It looks like a magazine, but its "articles" are related to the product being sold. Again, like the single-product package, an order form is included.

Polypak samples are wrapped samples of such items as binder cards, which are sold in a series. "Animals of the wild" and "Mom's recipes" are examples.

The advantages of direct mail, as a medium, include the following:

1. Selectivity of the names for the mailings
2. Personalized mail pieces
3. Low or no competition for attention during the promotion
4. Easy evaluation for effectiveness
5. Unique ability to provide stamps, ruboffs, name labels, and so on
6. Selection of format by the direct marketer (not limited to a TV screen, newspaper or magazine page, etc.)

The major disadvantage of direct mail is that it is a relatively expensive medium. It costs, on the average, 15 to 20 times more to reach a prospect through direct mail than through traditional media.

Electronic Media

Electronic media, which include both television and radio, are growing in popularity. Some direct marketers include computer services, such as the Internet, in the electronic media category; however, because of the differences in use and the growth of that particular medium, many treat it, as we do here, as a separate category. The idea behind electronic media is to provide ads that stimulate a direct response from the consumer. The advertisements should include a phone number and/or address for ordering the product or, at the very least, inquiring about it. Examples include electronic media advertisements for insurance policies, exercise equipment, and credit cards.

Many direct marketers are using another form of electronic media for their marketing: videocassettes. Videocassettes are sponsored by IMC planners who are trying to obtain leads or to make sales through direct marketing or the more traditional personal selling. Usually the ads are placed before a movie on a rented or purchased videotape, and a phone number is provided for the consumer to respond.

Print Media

Print media are familiar to most individual consumers because of the large extent of their daily exposure. Print media include newspapers (*The Wall Street Journal, USA Today,* local papers, etc.) or newspaper supplements (e.g., *Parade Magazine*) and professional, trade, and consumer publications, as well as free-standing inserts (FSIs). Newspaper and magazine ads are relatively inexpensive at the local level and can reach thousands of targeted people at the same time. The costs rise if the advertisements are placed in national or international newspaper or magazines. The cost of reaching the targeted audience varies, depending on where the ads are placed.

Free-standing inserts are a fairly inexpensive method of getting a direct marketing piece to its audience. The FSIs are created and printed by the marketer and then inserted "freely" into a newspaper or magazine. The term *freely* does not refer to a cost factor but to the fact that the inserts are not attached or bound to the magazine, newspaper, or other product. All FSIs should include a contact phone number or address to allow for an immediate response to the advertisement.

Outbound Telemarketing Calls

Outbound telephone calling is one form of telemarketing. It is similar to direct mail in that the names should be carefully selected before the phone-calling campaign. Names of prospects are usually rented and mixed with an in-house database to engender a complete calling list. Outbound telephone marketing has some of the advantages of direct mail, especially in the evaluation of results.

Miscellaneous Media

Many other types of media are utilized in direct marketing. For example, matchbooks, invoice inserts (bill stuffers), and cooperative card decks are fairly popular. Often matchbooks are sponsored by such advertisers as stamp suppliers for stamp collectors. The product or service is generally described on the outside cover, and an order blank for the product or service is printed on the inside.

Invoice inserts are little brochures that can be included with the statements sent to customers. You may have noticed them when receiving bills from credit card companies, utility companies, or catalog companies. The order forms are provided if you are asked to send your orders to a separate address; however, some marketers create ease of ordering by allowing the consumer to put the order form in with the payment.

Cooperative card decks (co-op decks) involve numerous marketers, who share the mailing costs for any given promotion. Advertisements from many different marketers are printed on index cards and placed together in a deck. The deck is then mailed to targeted audiences by the deck company. The disadvantage is that this type of direct marketing does not share in one of the major advantages of direct marketing—the reduction of clutter. With deck marketing, the clutter is delivered to the consumer. Many different advertisers can be present in any given deck. The advantage is the reduction in cost for reaching so many consumers.

DATABASE MARKETING

Before proceeding to tactics, some explanation of database marketing is necessary. Database marketing is used by both direct and indirect marketers. For direct marketing, the database is used to store information about customers and prospects. This information is then used to select the best names for a particular promotion. Many companies have in-house operational computer systems that fulfill orders for products. These systems are usually not designed for marketing decisions; rather, they are used to feed a computer marketing database. Such information as names, addresses, purchase data, payment data, and so on are transferred from the operational system. Many of these feeds from operational systems come together and create a marketing database.

A second source of information for the database comes from renting outside lists. Because many customers are interested in the same type of products, marketers rent names from other companies. The agreement usually states that the marketer can use the list one time at such-and-such a cost per thousand names. The actual amount depends on how much the list is in demand. For example, a hot list may include customers who have made recent purchases, say in the last three months, through the vehicle being used by the direct marketer. Names are very important in building customer lists and databases, so the benefit of having them outweighs the cost of the rental.

After the names have been added to the database, the next step is "list enhancement," the addition of other valuable demographic, psychographic, geographic, and behavioristic information. A very basic example is the addition of income and age, but this process can become much more sophisticated. Information may be added to the database that indicates the "number of males in the household interested in bass fishing during the summer months." List enhancement is accomplished in several different ways. The most popular method is to send in-house names to be matched to a demographic database that is maintained by a list compiler, such as Metromail/Donnelley or R. L. Polk & Company. The cost of this process is calculated on a "per hit" method of matching. Because this information may not belong to a marketer, he or she cannot rent the list to others.

Tactics

Tactics were described in some detail earlier in the chapter, but this is where decisions are being made about how to implement the strategy. After the strategic decision is made to utilize direct sales, direct response marketing, or both, the IMC planner must decide which tactics to use. In direct sales, the tactical decision is whether to use personal selling (covered in another chapter) or telemarketing. In direct-response marketing, the tactical decision is what type of direct response is the most effective (for response and costs), the choices being direct mail, print, television, radio, or a minor medium. The thing to keep in mind is that direct marketing must be integrated into and synergistic with the other areas of the IMC mix, as well as have an impact on the overall marketing plan.

The planner should also include samples of what the tactical executions will look like. If needed, a sample script from a telemarketing campaign is appropriate. Samples of any mail pieces should be included. Storyboards for infomercials are good, and perhaps an animatic could be included with the overall IMC plan to make sure that the advertiser or reader understands what the result will look like. In any case, samples help to sell the overall plan, as well as generate feedback from the advertiser about what the campaign can do.

Rationale

A rationale must be provided for all of the decisions made. It is also appropriate to create a direct marketing flowchart to indicate the times (days, months, quarters, etc.) and costs associated with the direct marketing plan. There should be a budget, outlining costs and expected outcomes. It is also important to indicate how the direct marketing mix fits in with the overall IMC mix and, ultimately, with the overall marketing mix and objectives. Graphs, flowcharts, and other methods of presenting the information should be included if appropriate. Finally, if direct marketing or specific areas of the plan have been rejected, it would be a good idea to tell the reader why those tactics or strategies weren't used.

EVALUATION

Because the results from direct marketing must be, by definition, measurable, it is probably the easiest IMC mix variable to evaluate, for two reasons: (1) purchases from direct marketing are typically more immediate than from mass advertising, and (2) purchases can be tracked to specific customers (unlike the purchases in, say, a supermarket). For example, if a marketer mails out 200,000 promotional pieces to prospects, and receives 4,500 orders, it is easy to say that the direct mailing had a 2.2 percent response rate. This evaluation is important when comparing different tactics. For instance, when deciding on two different outside lists to rent, if for budgetary reasons only one can be utilized, the list with the higher response rate would most likely be rented. In addition, by tracking the effectiveness of the direct marketing campaign, the marketer can make important strategic decisions on which methods to utilize in the future, based on success rates of the past. The marketer must be sure to develop an evaluative methodology to take advantage of this unique aspect. However, the marketer must also control and implement changes if certain tactics or strategies aren't working. The immediate tracking system in direct marketing allows for changes during a campaign. So, the marketer must take advantage of the evaluative uniqueness of direct marketing but make sure there is a system in place to address any ineffectiveness as it is measured. The evaluative methods help to sell the advertiser on the effectiveness and need for the direct marketing portion of the overall IMC plan.

Finally, some type of evaluative system should be in place to see that the direct marketing campaign is in line with all of the other IMC variables.

Figure 5–1 offers the chance to develop your own direct marketing plan. Insert your thoughts and ideas in the spaces provided, and at the end you'll have a comprehensive direct marketing plan.

FIGURE 5–1 The Direct Marketing Plan: A Template

Direct Marketing Objectives:

Strategies for Objective Attainment:

Media Selected:

Tactical Executions (List and Provide Sample Executions):

Campaign Rationale:

Evaluative and Control Methods:

CHAPTER

Cybermarketing 6

With technologies growing at increasing rates, there has also been a growth in the use of computer-based marketing. Although very new, computer-based marketing, or *cybermarketing,* is growing quickly, with many marketers trying to take advantage of the new technologies to reach consumers. Once associated with advertising, this type of IMC has become so large that it now is considered a separate category.

The objective of cybermarketing is to use the power of online networks, computer communications, and digital interactive media to reach a targeted audience or to enhance marketing objectives. When utilizing this IMC variable mix, it is important to keep these objectives in mind. Although cybermarketing won't fix all of the problems associated with IMC, it will add more interactivity.

There is overlap between cybermarketing and the other areas of the IMC mix. For example, cybermarketing can use traditional media to generate sales leads (direct marketing) for a particular product or event. Movie producers have included Internet addresses for many of their recent products in order to stimulate consumer interest in and demand for some of the new shows that are being introduced to the market. Realizing that the overlap exists is essential for good cybermarketing development.

OBJECTIVES AND STRATEGIES

The IMC planner must decide where and if cybermarketing will fit into the IMC mix. Cybermarketing can reduce, or remove dependence on paper and add more information to the IMC mix. It can also remove certain barriers in reaching targeted audiences. It is important for the marketer to realize that there are limitations to what can be accomplished with this type of marketing. The evaluation of cybermarketing, although seemingly easy, is quite difficult. Why then, would you use cybermarketing as part of the IMC campaign?

- Traditional marketing and advertising are often expensive (brochures, product sheets, catalogs, etc.). Cybermarketing gives the advantage of additional reach and frequency without a lot of the costs associated with traditional methods.
- Traditional marketing and advertising can be time-intensive (e.g., while correcting mistakes and making revisions).
- Traditional marketing and advertising have a more hit-or-miss quality (e.g., telephone tag and direct mail).

Again, cybermarketing won't fix all of the problems in the other areas of IMC, but it can add interactivity. The objectives for cybermarketing must follow the rules for the other mix variables. They must be achievable, measurable, and realistic.

Because there are many types of cybermarketing, it may be best to develop objectives for each of the strategic decisions and tactical executions. The following list provides the major different types of cybermarketing:

1. Creating a CD-ROM
2. E-mail marketing
3. Electronic data interchange
4. Business-oriented database services
5. Posting, hosting or presenting information on the Internet

Each of these cybermarketing types is discussed in detail.

TYPES OF CYBERMARKETING

Creating a CD-ROM

The objectives of a CD-ROM are the following:

1. To reduce the costs of printing, storing, and shipping of large volumes of data to customers and prospects
2. To make a sale by using interactive, visual formats rather than by presenting a complex sales story
3. To reduce the printing cost of updating customer support reference materials

You can create your own CD-ROM for approximately five cents per megabyte of information. A CD-ROM disc is capable of holding 660 megabytes of data, the equivalent of around one-half million pages of text. In addition, you can add sound, animation, and still or moving video images.

The CD-ROM discs are recorded on compact disc-recordable drives, which sell for approximately $3,000. The software needed to master and premaster the discs adds an additional $1,000 to $2,500 to the total costs (but these costs are beginning to come down).

Premastering is the process of converting data into a format that is accepted by standard CD-ROM drives. Premastering requires a significant amount of computer storage space (up to 640 megabytes). Most premastering software packs support tape drives, as well as hard-drive options for storing. For the beginner, three of the most popular software packages for premastering are CD-Prepare, CD-Record, and Tempra CD Maker.

The marketer must decide which form the actual compact disc will take. For example, a text-only CD is less expensive and time-consuming than other types. However, to adds attention, interest, desire, and action (the AIDA model), the marketer may want to add other media to provide support for the text (sound, images, interactivity, etc.). Software for only text is different from software utilized for multimedia applications.

In creating a CD-ROM, you should do the following:

- Use new technologies. These are more effective and interesting to your audience than are text-only or printed versions of the same material.

- Offer interactivity, if possible. Consumers are more apt to make purchases once they become involved in the process.
- In some instances, a provision for printing may be required. Some customers like to generate hard copies of materials.
- Give customers the ability to access the information and data quickly.
- Make the CD-ROM easy to update and modify.
- Avoid heavy and long copy.

Because of the strides in CD technology, more and more customers will be utilizing the medium. As use increases, the value of CD-ROMs also increases. Don't overlook the potential marketing value of this technology.

The CD-ROM could be distributed at trade shows, mailed to prospects, used to support personal selling, or distributed as a sales promotional item (perhaps in lieu of a gift or business card).

E-Mail Marketing

Electronic mail, or E-mail, is the system used to deliver messages, via some communication network, from one computer to another (or series of others). Instead of paper-based tools such as memos, letters, and so on, E-mail can be used. E-mail is one of the fastest growing areas in the high-tech industry.

What are the advantages of E-mail?

- Because of its digital format, information can be managed on screen, thus eliminating hard copy.
- Delivery occurs instantaneously.
- It is relatively inexpensive.
- It is reliable.
- Messages can be stored without taking up additional space or requiring filing.
- It allows filtering. The user can quickly scan the messages to see which is important. However, this is also a disadvantage to the marketer because it allows the user to skip his or her message.

Electronic Data Interchange

Electronic data interchange (EDI) enables communicators to exchange business documents electronically. A marketer could set up electronic networks with vendors or customers to reduce the amount of paper that has to flow between them.

When EDI is used as an ordering system, it can reduce the time required to place an order and receive shipments of products. For the marketer, the advantages to utilizing an EDI system are to:

- Expand the customer base
- Provide customer service
- Expand the supplier base
- Reduce paperwork (documents)
- Increase problem recognition and resolution
- Increase customer service

For the IMC planner, the advantages of providing for and expanding customer service may be the most important. For the business-to-business IMC planner, the expansion of a customer base and the provision for problem recognition may be the most important. In planning IMC for a large company that has a significant amount of volume, EDI may be an option. For smaller organizations, an EDI system may not have the associated benefits.

Business-Oriented Database Services

Business-oriented database services are gateways for information and data. Essentially, they digitize news wire services, technical databases, newspapers, and so on, and make them available via a computer and modem.

Business-oriented database services are focused on businesses, not end users. They charge a high fee for the service and focus mainly on providing information, not the process of communication. However, the IMC planner may be able to use these systems to assist in communication by providing clients with data on industry news. They could help track business or consumer trends and, through large background searches, help generate information that will impress your clients or potential clients.

The following are some of the major players in business-oriented database services:

- CLARITAS CATALYST CONNECT
- DATATIMES
- DIALOG

Each of these services specializes in the type of information that it carries. For the most part, demographic data, as well as census and business information, can be downloaded from these sources.

The Internet

The U.S. Department of Defense, around 1965, financed the development of a computer network that has evolved into the Internet. The idea was to link a handful of universities and military research laboratories. Today the system has thousands of connections, via leased telephone lines, in over 100 countries.

The Internet has thousands of interconnected networks, linking over 4 million computers around the world. The technology and usage is so new that estimates tell us that a major network links onto the Internet every 30 minutes. For those not familiar with Internet terminology, appendix F lists some basic terms used in cyberspace.

Internet users can gain access to the World Wide Web (WWW) in one of three ways. First, they can subscribe to a commercial online service such as America Online (AOL) or Prodigy. They can connect through an Internet service provider (ISP), or they can operate their own Web server, becoming a local or regional ISP. Most users begin with a basic subscription plan. Why is this important to you as the IMC planner? More than 10 million Americans subscribe to commercial online services. It is important that you are able to reach these individuals to communicate your message.

Small, as well as large, businesses can generate connections to the Internet, utilizing an Internet provider. The four main levels of connection are the following:

Gateway. This is a bulletin board service or consumer-oriented online service like Prodigy or AOL. With this type of account, the user is utilizing the service provider's computer to gain access. In other words, the user is not on the Web in the strictest sense.

Dial-up. This is also called a terminal or shell account. It allows the user to view files on the Internet. These accounts are not on the Internet—they are using the service provider's host system—but are important audience members for IMC planners.

SLIP. This account gives faster access to the Internet but at a greater cost to the user.

High-speed dedicated lines. These provide the fastest, and generally the easiest, access to the Internet.

If the IMC planner decides to utilize service providers, a number of things are important to take full advantage of the service:

1. Your provider should offer a full range of basic Internet applications (newsgroups, mailing lists, E-mail, etc.), including the ability to utilize search tools and multimedia on the WWW.
2. Be sure that the provider has no confining restrictions on use.
3. The provider should have a marketing focus on the services being offered.
4. Check costs.
5. Be sure there is good backup service.
6. Be sure you can get good technical support.

With a basic understanding of the Internet, as an IMC planner, it's up to you to provide plans for your clients to utilize the WWW. Many valuable applications to IMC help sell products over WWW. For example, many marketers are utilizing *cybermalls,* essentially online shopping sites in which merchants showcase their goods and services. The IMC planner may also want to create his or her own website.

Before creating your own website or the website for a client, do some homework. Surf the Web: Decide which sites are the most attractive. What are other companies doing for website development? Which sites are generating the most hits or are most successful? A commercial website must be available to customers or potential customers nonstop, that is, 24 hours a day, all year round. If a customer dials up your website and there is no answer, you've just lost a sale.

To publish and list information on the Internet, you need a full-time, dedicated Internet connection. In addition, you need to obtain and install your Web server, which is done by using software developed for this purpose. Be sure you register your universal resource locator (URL). Generate a creative name for your address but one that provides some type of information about what you or your client does.

Some dangers are involved with the development of websites for clients. The first rule of thumb, before deciding if you even want a website, is to **know the customers.** This refers to your clients as well as to the product's end user. If the customers are businesspeople, it would be best to develop time-saving, clean, geographically appealing websites that don't have long download times. Thus remember that if you're adding glitz to the site, you're also increasing download time. It has been estimated that the addition of audio, video, graphic animation, and other components increases site costs by 20 to 50 percent, as well as the time required for downloading. Focus site development on the customer. By adhering to the four following suggestions, you have a good starting point for developing an attractive website.

Offer Information Make it easy for the targeted audiences to find out about your products and services. Remember, the reason they're on the Web is to get a lot of information in a short period of time. Give easy categories. Be sure the message is clear and that there are no grammatical or typographical errors. Allow for customer service via the site. In other words, follow all good marketing and communication rules when developing the site—it serves as a representation of the company, as well as a silent salesperson.

Empower the Customer   Allow ease of downloading. Attach answers to often-asked questions about the product or service. Provide an E-mail address to allow the customer to communicate with service personnel or salespeople who can provide additional information if this is required.

Upgrade and Care for the Site   Be sure all information is accurate and up to date and that prices are current. Be sure that all communication on the site is integrated into and synergistic with the information being provided to the audience through the other cybermarketing and IMC vehicles. Always identify each page in case the customer didn't enter through the home page. Follow the basic communication concept of AIDA: Create attention, generate interest, inspire desire, and ask for and provide for some type of action. This can be accomplished by offering incentives to the targeted audience.

Answer Your E-mail   Just providing an E-mail address on the site is not enough. You must answer the E-mail in a prompt and professional manner. If you cannot answer questions about the product or service or provide additional information to the customer, stay off the Web.

One of the strengths of the Internet is the ability to deliver real-time prices better than a CD-ROM or print media. The trick to developing a good cybermarketing plan is to play to the strength of each communication channel. CD-ROMs may offer better images and provide fast access. Thus, a fashion show for clothing would probably be better suited to a CD-ROM than to a website. Print, on the other hand, may offer a longer life and higher resolution than a CD-ROM.

The following process may help in website development. Use it as a suggested course of action.

- *Planning.*   Choose the best Web server. In other words, who provides the best access to the targeted audiences? What type of information must be collected? Updated? What resources will be needed to construct and support the operation of the site?
- *Analysis.*   This is the process of gathering and comparing information about the Web and its ability to improve overall quality and communication. This would also include the analysis of competitors' sites.
- *Design.*   What is the Web's purpose? What audiences are to be reached? Is there synergy with the other IMC variables?
- *Implementation.*   Build the web site by using hypertext markup language (HTML).
- *Promotion.*   Be sure that every potential customer is aware of the website. Create public relations. Promote the use of the site.
- *Innovation.*   Always review, evaluate, and control the effectiveness of this vehicle for the client or your company. Monitor new innovations or technologies that may have an impact on your products or services. Improve the quality of the website whenever possible.

Finally, since we have a list of what should be done, we need to provide a list of what shouldn't be done when creating websites.

- ***Don't use all of the budget for site construction.***   There has to be innovation or upgrades for the site, so allow some reserve funds in the budget. Remember, upgrades cost money.
- ***Don't create promotions that are too wide.***   Narrowly define the targeted audience.
- ***Don't treat online and offline promotions in the same way.***   Online customers can say no by simply hitting the "Back" button. Be sure you have a close.
- ***Get closure.***   Make the Web surfers register or send for free material, product information, offline communication—anything to keep them from surfing away.

- *Realize that there is a difference between net sales and net marketing.* The use of a website is really to help communicate your message. It is needed, but it may not generate sales. It may provide information. Think of it as a necessity, such as a fax machine or telephone, more than as a salesperson. It assists in generating income, but is not the main source.
- *Don't obsess over a domain name.*
- *Don't design for yourself.*
- *Don't try to save money by getting a cheap Web host.*
- *Don't exclude technical staff from planning.*
- *Don't provide information that no one reads or is interested in.*
- *Follow the KISS principle:* **K**eep **I**t **S**imple, Stupid.

TACTICS

After the development of the objectives and strategies for cybermarketing, develop the tactics. Give examples of what is to be done. Actual mockups of home pages or websites would be helpful. In addition, sample CD-ROMs might help sell the advertisers and marketers on the whole cybermarketing role. If E-mail is to be used, be sure to provide the copy.

The following list shows some features that help make the use of CD-ROM important in developing an effective IMC platform:

Multimedia. CD-ROM discs can provide full-color graphics, charts, drawings, and photographs to generate high impact. Work up tactical executions that highlight these advantages.

Customer control. Prospects want only certain information, and CD-ROMs can be organized to provide it. Again, when developing the tactical executions, provide samples that highlight this advantage.

Inexpensive shipping. The CD-ROMs are relatively inexpensive to ship. Compared to a catalog or heavy brochure, they are postal money savers. The IMC planner may want to include samples of CD-ROM mailers.

More multimedia. The CD-ROMs may include animation, video, audio, music, and sound effects. Samples should be developed and included with the IMC plan to show the advertiser what can be done with additional monies.

Flexibility. The CD-ROMs can be used to achieve a number of different marketing objectives, including new product introductions, user education programs, sales presentations, and so on. They are extremely helpful as a supplement to advertising and public relations or as a sales promotion tool.

When developing E-mail as a potential IMC method, also remember to include samples of how it can be used. Perhaps E-mail formats, copy, and so on could be included in this portion of the IMC plan.

RATIONALE

As in any of the areas of IMC, a rationale must be provided for the use of any or all of the cybermarketing methods. A cost flowchart would be helpful to the reader to assess the basic benefits of cybermarketing.

EVALUATION

All methods of cybermarketing used must be evaluated. The evaluation can be based on objective outcomes. If objectives are not being met, the IMC planner must understand why. It is also important to control for the ineffectiveness of the cybermarketing campaign. Problems should be addressed and fixed as soon as they are discovered.

Cybermarketing has a built-in evaluation system that can be used as a rough measure of effectiveness. The computer systems can monitor and measure the number of hits that each of the various vehicles provides. These hits provide a rough measure of the number of people reached by the cybermarketing message, although additional research is needed to understand the frequencies associated with each. Needless to say, this should not be the only measure of evaluation, although it does provide a reliable rough measurement.

Fill in Figure 6–1 with your cybermarketing program. Make sure that there is integration with all of the other IMC variable mixes. Provide a flowchart that shows when cybermarketing marketing activities are occurring, that reaches figures, and that indicates the costs of the program.

FIGURE 6–1 The Cybermarketing Plan: A Template

Objectives:

Strategy:

Tactical Executions:

Rationale:

Evaluative Methods:

The Cybermarketing Flowchart:

CHAPTER

Personal Selling
7

Personal selling involves person-to-person communication. The seller attempts to persuade an individual to purchase products from his or her company. Personal selling used to require face-to-face communication, but in recent years it has expanded to the use of electronic communication, primarily the telephone. The most important aspect of personal selling is personal interaction and communication. It should be obvious, then, that personal selling is different from the other IMC variables in that it involves small numbers of consumers (in many cases, just one buyer) rather than many (in advertising, many millions may be exposed to the message).

The sales function is typically housed under the vice president or manager of sales. It is not, for most organizations, a line of responsibility for the marketing manager. Some organizations, however, do use the umbrella of sales and marketing as one job function. This is the ideal model for building integrated marketing because selling is related to all other communication functions and should fall under this category.

The primary disadvantage of personal selling is its cost per contact. Whereas advertising communicates to large numbers of consumers (or potential consumers), salespeople communicate to small numbers, in many cases, just one person.

Some advantages of personal selling include the ability to customize messages. The customized package could include sales pitches designed specifically for the customer's interests. Feedback is immediate with personal selling. The salesperson can understand if the pitch is working or if the presentation needs some modification for a particular customer. Personal selling also allows the salesperson the ability to show and tell; in other words, product demonstration is possible, thus increasing the chances for a sale. Attention from the customer is another advantage. Because the communication is face to face, the customer has a hard time avoiding the salesperson's message. Coupled with feedback, this is a powerful tool. Finally, personal selling allows for the development of customer continuity. The salesperson can develop a long-term relationship with the buyer, again facilitating sales.

Many types of activities occur in the sales process. It is important that the IMC planner understand each one so that the entire IMC plan can be scheduled with efficiency. Following is a list of the major types of sales activities. They must be scheduled to occur in a preplanned process to make the integrated marketing effective and balanced.

- *Trade selling.* Trade selling emphasizes increased sales volume through promotional assistance to customers. There is a direct connection with the sales promotion function for which the sales plan must provide.
- *Missionary selling.* Missionary selling emphasizes sales for the benefit of the direct customer. The missionary salesperson is attempting to create goodwill for the

company, while at the same time trying to generate future sales. There are no direct sales associated with this activity.

- *New business selling.* Sometimes called cold calling, this activity is a continuous process in which the sales staff tries to obtain new accounts. Advertisers call this function business development.
- *Retail selling.* Here the customer comes in direct contact with a salesperson at a retail outlet. The customer, in this case, comes to the salesperson with a specific need or want to be satisfied. The salespeople are sometimes referred to as order takers.
- *Telemarketing.* In telemarketing, the telephone is used to perform many of the sales functions (i.e., order taking or order getting).

In addition to these sales activities, many methods are utilized in personal selling. The three most common methods are *hard selling, soft selling,* and *consultative selling.* All methods have the same end in mind, that is, to close or make a sale, but they use different approaches.

In *hard selling,* the salesperson tries to convince the customer to make a deal. This method is concerned with making the sale, rather than trying to identify the consumer's wants and needs and then satisfying them. The customer is viewed almost as an opponent rather than as a partner. No mutual satisfaction is involved in this process.

Soft selling attempts to make the process of hard selling easier. The soft sell tries to make the customer perceive the purchase of goods and services as less risky than it actually may be. The soft seller attempts to ease the customer into the relationship by avoiding initial risk to the buyer. Free estimates, samples, demonstrations, and consultations are a number of tactics used by the soft salesperson. In soft selling it is important to provide the customer with enough data so that the buyer can get to know the company or product, commonly through pamphlets, brochures, videotapes, and audiotapes. The idea is to make the consumer understand that the next logical step in the process is the purchase of the product or service.

Consultative selling is an advanced form of friendly persuasion. The salesperson needs to gain the customers' confidence by assisting them in finding profitable solutions to their problems. The development of a relationship is the major goal of consultative selling, which is generally profit for both. The process of consultative selling has four steps: (1) Identify the customer's problem. (2) Identify how much the customer can spend to solve the problem. (3) Solve the problem in terms of benefits to the customer (the biggest benefit is increased profits). Don't push the product on the customer; instead suggest solutions. (4) Realize that you, as the salesperson, are in control of the solution. With this in mind, propose a partnership and close the sale.

Just as with the other IMC variables, a plan must be developed for the personal selling function. The plan should include discussions and information on just how the function fits in with the other variables. There must be coordination in each of the departments, especially if sales is a separate function from the rest of the integrated marketing areas.

OBJECTIVES

The first step in the development of a good sales plan is to list the objectives. Often the objectives can be secured from the manager or vice president of sales. These objectives must fit in with the other IMC objectives and must flow from the overall objectives set forth in the IMC plan. If the objectives are not available, the sales planner must decide what the function of personal selling will be during the campaign. All objectives (including advertising, sales, promotion, etc.) must be communicated to anyone and everyone involved in the IMC process. Sales objectives must be measurable to ensure that the sales function is productive. In addition, budgets should be assigned to the sales function: How much should be spent on this important area?

STRATEGY

A sales strategy is the next step in producing an effective and integrated sales plan: What is the big picture? How will we achieve the objectives that were set? Often the strategy can be generated from the sales practices of the firm. Because the firm is customer-focused and employs the marketing concept as a guide for doing business, consultative selling may be effectively utilized. The strategic area should include information on territory assignments, costs, and options for strategic change if the chosen strategies appear to be ineffective. It would be appropriate to include a schedule of sales target dates to allow coordination with the other IMC variables. A sales chart, indicating when sales groups should be calling on customers, how often, and when, is a tool that will make the job of integration much easier for the planner.

TACTICS

Sales tactics are the actual executions of the sales plan, the personal selling activity. There are numerous types of sales tactics, usually involving one or more of the methods of selling previously discussed. The main point is that planning creates sales.

It has been said that the successful function of selling depends on preparation, rather than actual presentation. The salesperson who prepares the presentation before delivering it is much more successful than the one who just delivers. The sales plan must be developed to meet the needs of the customer. Because the marketing concept deals with meeting customer needs, at a profit, so should the sales plan. Do not sell for the moment. Remember, repeat customers are the life blood of any organization or business. It is easier and much cheaper to retain a customer than to generate new business. With this in mind, a good sales manager, in conjunction with his or her sales staff, will develop a plan for each and every step in the sales process. The plan should not be memorized. It should be logical. It should be an outline, not a speech.

Following is an outline that should help you develop a sales plan. Use it as a guide in preparing the information necessary for the sales function to work. Remember, it must be integrated into all the other areas of marketing to engender a successful campaign. The sales staff should be able to pick up the outline and find it useful. It should not be a major work but rather a guide. Follow the KISS principle, and "keep it simple, stupid."

A SAMPLE SALES PLAN OUTLINE

1. The Preapproach Plan
   a. Describe the attitude necessary for the successful completion of the sale.
   b. Describe the appropriate appearance. This step is essential in developing rapport with the prospective customer. Most decisions about the company and sales representative are made within the first few minutes. Personal appearance plays a major role in the customer's thoughts and decisions about you.
   c. Describe your company. In addition, list the major competitors. What are the major sales appeals of all those involved in the industry? Provide a Strengths,

Weaknesses, Opportunities, and Threats (SWOT) analysis of each of the competing products.

d. Describe the features of the products. Turn the features into benefits. Include information about pricing for your product, as well as for those of the competitors.

e. Provide a detailed explanation of the typical prospect. If possible, utilize research to provide data on the current prospects. Are they typical? What are their likes and dislikes? How do they buy?

f. List as many reasons for buying (for the typical prospect) as possible. Be inclusive. Any ideas that may help in the sales process should be listed. Don't delete ideas because you may think that they're stupid.

g. Secure a sales promotion piece on the products that are going to be sold.

h. Secure any types of integrated marketing that may be used to assist in the sales of the product. For example, if advertising is to be used, get copies of the storyboards. Better yet, get animatics or actual carts of the advertisements. If POPs are going to be used, get examples of those.

i. Get any product information sheets available to use in the sales process.

2. Develop the Presale Plan

a. What should be said in the sales presentation? Don't provide a canned speech unless the strategy calls for hard or soft selling. Highlight the major features and benefits of the product. Also, include information that should be given in the opening few minutes of the presentation.

b. Decide what you will do during the sales presentation. You don't have to follow this step by step, but have a good idea of what activities you will undertake. For example, do you plan to demonstrate the product? Will you take the buyer to lunch? Will you have only three minutes of the buyer's time, thus requiring you to get to the point immediately?

c. Preplan opening questions.

d. Preplan follow-up questions. What questions will you use to explore the needs and wants of the customer? What questions can you develop that will help to create a positive relationship with the potential customer?

e. Go over the presentation strategy. What should be accomplished at the first meeting and subsequent meetings with the customer?

f. Plan the demonstration.
   i. Will you demonstrate the product?
   ii. Will the demonstration occur onsite or elsewhere?
   iii. What features or, better yet, benefits will be demonstrated to the customer?
   iv. What sales aids are required to complete the demonstration? (Be sure you've secured all that are needed.)

g. Plan how to overcome buyer objections.
   i. List the most common objections that the buyer will bring up.
   ii. List any other objections you can think of.
   iii. List specific ways to overcome these objections.

h. Prepare a list of closing clues to look for.

i. Go over the various closing techniques. Choose the one that you think will work the best. Then list, in order of effectiveness, all of the other closing techniques that could be utilized by the sales staff.

j. Suggestion sell. Develop a plan to sell additional items to the customer. How will these items be brought up? What items are available to compliment the main purchase? For example, could you sell an extended warranty for a high-tech product? How about an a tie or shirt to complement the suit that was just purchased?

    k. Is delivery needed? How will this be undertaken?

    l. Is installation needed? How will this be undertaken? Will there be an additional charge to install the automatic ice-maker that you gave away as a sales promotion item to the customer? Will this additional charge anger the customer? If so, how will this be handled?

    m. What postsale activities will you be involved in? If it's a good customer, will you make a courtesy call to see that all is well with the purchase? What about the mailing of birthday cards? How does this tie in to the sales promotion aspects of the IMC plan?

3. Present the actual sale

    a. What presentation will you use?

    b. How will you follow up?

    c. How will you document the sales call? What kind of evaluative methodology will help the next call?

    d. Note whether the sale was made. If not, what has been learned?

4. Prepare a list of costs associated with the sales presentation. Were these expenses needed? Were they effective? Could they be transferred to other selling situations with other customers? Could they be discarded?

5. Generate a budget for the sales plan.

6. Evaluate the overall effectiveness of the sales call. Were the objectives met? What could be done more effectively? What could be reworked? What are those things that worked that could be transferred to other salespeople? Other departments?

7. Rehearse. Develop methods to allow the sales representatives to practice their presentations. Develop a method to critique them. Videotaping is usually an effective method. Perhaps joining select salespeople on sales calls and then providing constructive comments may help. This rehearsal method should be preplanned and implemented to allow for greater sales generation. Don't wait until the last minute. Every customer is a potential sale.

It is important to remember that major functions are involved in sales management. Although it is not the function of this book to help improve sales management, note that the IMC planner must realize that the sales manager has a number of responsibilities. These include: (1) organizing resources (human and capital), (2) recruiting staff, (3) leading, (4) motivating, (5) training, (6) managing information, and (7) supervising. Without these functions, the sales variable will not be effective. When working with the personnel in selling, keep these activities in mind and be empathetic.

RATIONALE

Once the sales functions have been planned, a rationale must be provided for each activity. Why are we using consultative selling? Hard selling? Soft selling? Why are we undertaking an increase in the personal selling function? The rationale should be extended to include all areas of the sales function. In other words, reasons should be given for final consumer sales, as well as business-to-business sales. For example, a rationale should be provided for why a manager is using, say, missionary selling and how it fits into the IMC plan.

A rationale should be provided for the timetables, budgets, and personnel involved in the sales function. Finally, how does this function create the synergy needed in the successful completion of the IMC plan?

EVALUATION

The personal selling function must also include methods for evaluation. The effectiveness of selling must be noted. At face value, it may seem easy to evaluate the sales staff; however, this isn't always the case. Although one good evaluative tool for personal selling is how much each salesperson is bringing in, environmental influences may affect that bottom-line figure. For example, there may have been inadequate sales training or the economy may have taken a downward turn. There may not be enough salespeople in a particular territory for effective coverage. Whatever the case, when evaluating the sales outcomes, be sure to understand the big picture before making many changes in the overall plan.

Figure 7–1 will help you develop the personal selling variable of the IMC plan. Fill in the blanks with the needed information. It may also be a good idea to generate a separate sales plan. Although this may not be the function of your job, it will help with the integration of all IMC areas, as well as the many activities of the selling function.

FIGURE 7–1 The Personal Selling Plan: A Template

Objectives:

Strategy:

Tactics (Include, If Wanted, a Sales Presentation Plan):

Rationale:

Evaluation:

CHAPTER

Public Relations and Publicity

8

The roles of public relations and publicity differ among various corporations and organizations. The use of these two variables is important to the integrated marketing planner and will affect the outcome of the IMC plan. Before proceeding, it would be a good idea to define what is meant by public relations and publicity.

Public relations, in the broadest sense, is the function of generating goodwill toward a company or organization. This function focuses on the relationships that are created between an organization and its public—for example, suppliers (or other channel members), employees, stockholders, or even the general population. In fact, the public could also include the competition. Anyone who may affect the company or whom the company may affect is a member of the public or a stakeholder. These people have a stake in what occurs at the company.

Public relations (PR) uses the media to communicate with the general public; thus it is somewhat like advertising. A major difference, however, is that PR is not paid for in the traditional sense. In other words, PR doesn't purchase air time from broadcast media or space from print media, as advertisers do. Rather, PR managers rely on newsworthy events to get their ideas placed in the media. Because of this, PR is not truly controllable. The media may or may not provide coverage of an event that is deemed important by an organization. In addition, PR may not always be positive, as advertising is. The media may generate negative PR, or "badwill" for an organization. Because members of the public know that an advertiser is the originator of a message, they may be skeptical of the message being communicated. However, the general public does not perceive the company as the sender of PR messages, so these may have more impact on the consumer than would a traditional advertisement.

Publicity is a subfunction of public relations. The function of publicity is to generate news about the organization, an individual in the organization, a product or service, or some newsworthy event that the PR department has developed. Publicity is viewed as free, although it does have costs. Because of its low cost and its ability to generate awareness of events or activities, there is a great return on its investment.

Publicity needs to be controlled or planned. It must be integrated into the entire IMC campaign. Unplanned messages delivered by the media should be limited or, ideally, eliminated. It is the job of the PR manager to make sure that this is the case. Although it would be nice to control all publicity, the fact of the matter is that this is impossible.

Much of the PR activity can be classified according to where it is aimed. For example, any PR activity aimed toward the end user can be classified as *consumer public relations*. Likewise, if the PR is aimed at the trade, it can be classified as *trade public relations*. The planning for both of these types of PR is similar in that the process of identifying objectives, strategies, and tactics is still followed. The difference lies in the tactics for each of these areas. Some media reach the trade much more effectively than the end user, and vice versa.

It should also be pointed out that there is overlap in the PR functions with those of the other IMC variables. For example, there are times when a firm may wish to advertise its public relations. These ads may be generated to reach important members of the public such as the government, customers, or voters. Also, not-for-profit groups or charities may wish to promote sponsored programs in order to generate goodwill or, for that matter, attendance at events. *Public relations advertising* is a good vehicle to use for that purpose.

Finally, there has been a move to reclassify public relations into *corporate public relations* and *marketing public relations*. Marketing PR generally is used in larger, consumer-oriented firms. The main focus is to provide support for the sales functions. In corporate public relations, the main premise is to focus on nonmarketing communication goals and activities. Both of these types of PR will have a direct effect on the communication outcomes and must be considered by the integrated marketing planner.

Whether we're dealing with trade or consumer public relations, we can have a number of different objectives. The major objectives generally fall into one of the following categories:

1. *Reputation management.*   The PR professionals attempt to create and manage the reputation of the organization.
2. *Lobbying.*   Sometimes referred to as public affairs management (because of the negative connotation of the term *lobbying*); this is the management of the communications of elected officials or regulatory bodies. The PR professionals may want to inform government leaders of certain activities and how these activities contribute to the public good. Perhaps the PR department wants to influence government bodies to oppose attempts at limiting a firm's activities or a new piece of legislation that may hurt the company or the public good.
3. *Special events management.*   This is the management of events that have been planned in the IMC plan. Sports marketing and sponsorships of cultural events are two major areas that may require some management. The events must be tied in with the other marketing communication activities, or the money expended for them is essentially wasted.
4. *Speech writing.*   Another function of the PR department is the creation of speeches for various organizational personnel. Any representative of a company must provide information to the public that is consistent with those messages being provided by the other IMC variables. The PR writers may also prepare answers to questions that are asked of the company's speakers.
5. *Publication development.*   The PR department is often required to develop and produce the many publications that are put out by an organization, for example, annual reports, brochures, or manuals. It is important that the message in the publications is consistent with the overall IMC message.

Public relations planning and development must follow the same logical steps that are followed by the other areas of IMC. All of the various members of the public who are receiving the communications from the company must be given the same message. The goals for PR must be written to achieve the overall marketing goals.

TRADE PUBLIC RELATIONS

Objectives   The first step in the creation of the trade PR plan is to develop specific objectives. Again, these must be measurable and achievable. They must also be synergistic with the consumer PR messages. It is important to note that the objectives for trade public relations may or may not be the same as those developed for the final consumer.

Strategies   To achieve the objectives, the PR planner must develop strategies. For the trade, reputation management seems to be the popular strategic approach. Certainly, speech writing and publications are also important strategic decision areas.

Tactics   To undertake the various strategic approaches decided on, the PR manager must develop tactics that will be effective. For reputation management, the PR manager may wish to employ publicity. Other tactical executions could be speech writing, press agentry, crisis management, or perhaps publications development. Whatever tactics are chosen, examples of each approach should be given in this section. For example, a sample speech may help to illustrate how the message will be communicated to the various trade audiences. The audience members want to know why and how the new actions by the firm will benefit them. They don't want or need to know superfluous information and data. Keep the speech focused on the audience. Similarly, a sample of an annual plan will show the document in a positive light.

Rationale   Any undertaking must have a rationale behind it. A flowchart could indicate who will be reached, and when, how, why, and where. The flowchart will show estimated costs and give a graphic example of what is to be undertaken and why. Any individual that will be involved in the public relations campaign should also be identified. It is a good idea to provide a time line for the roll-out of the PR campaign. This time line can then be coordinated with the other IMC variables to provide a powerful tool in convincing the decision makers of the need for these activities.

Evaluation   Some kind of evaluative tool must be used to assess the effectiveness of the trade PR campaign. Without any indication of effectiveness, the planner will not know if the tactics and strategies should be used again (or if the individuals executing the plan should be used again). Remember, the idea is to develop a hard-to-copy PR plan that effectively communicates to the targeted audiences and, at the same time, is totally integrated into the other areas of IMC.

CONSUMER PUBLIC RELATIONS

Objectives   As with trade PR, specific objectives need to be developed in dealing with the final consumer. The consumer should not be receiving messages that are different than those given to the trade and the public, but the messages should be targeted specifically to the end user. The objectives need to be time-specific, realistic, and measurable. Most of them should deal with marketing-oriented public relations (sometimes called MPR).

Strategies   Many strategies and tactics are involved in consumer public relations. The overall strategic goal is to deal with only marketing-related PR. Thomas L. Harris, in *The Marketer's Guide to Public Relations* (1993), identified three specific strategies for this type of PR: push, pass, and pull. The push strategy refers to trade public relations and to the firm trying to "push" the product or service through the channel of distribution. In a typical pull strategy, the consumer is asked to "pull" the product through the channel of distribution by requesting intermediaries to carry the product; for example, if the marketers can generate enough press, they can incite the potential consumers of sports sponsorships or other events. In utilizing the pass strategy, the marketer bypasses the traditional barriers to product introduction. Tactics would be developed to get around public interest groups, for example, to successfully launch a product.

Tactics   Numerous tactics are used by PR managers. The following list contains many (but not all) of the more popular tactics.

- *News releases* (also called press releases).   A news release consists of a small number of typed sheets (usually one or two) of information about an event, service, or product launch. The event must be summarized and must catch the media's attention or it is of little use. The news release is the most widely utilized public relations tool. A number of publications provide information on how to write an effective news release.

- *Photographs.*   Photos are used to generate attention and create excitement for newsworthy events. There should always be typed captions with the photos, and if individuals are pictured (which is a good idea) they should be identified (sometimes on the back of the picture). Often photographs are included with or attached to the main news release.

- *Media kits* (or press kits).   The media kit includes the basic news release, photos, and additional information about an event. Often a fact sheet is included, as well as expanded information about the people involved in the event. It is not unusual to find a schedule of events in the media kit. Many organizations, mostly those involved in motion picture marketing, have developed an electronic press kit, which includes a videotape of the event and clips that can be broadcast. Also included is a fact sheet about the clips and how and when to use them. News stations that review movies and reviewers like Siskel and Ebert receive electronic press kits to help them show the better parts of a movie. This encourages a better review and gives the public a demonstration of what the movie is about.

- *Fact sheets.*   These are similar to a news release, except they just contain factual information about the event, product, or service. The idea is to induce the media into writing a feature article about the event. Also, the fact sheet may clear up any misunderstandings about a product, event, or service by providing factual information and data.

- *Feature articles.*   Many of the media will develop and run feature stories or articles about some event (or product or service). Here the feature article would be written by a professional writer employed by an organization. The key to writing a feature article for publication or broadcast is to make it timeless so that the editor can broadcast or print the story whenever there is time or room to do so. Some features may include case histories or how to do something.

- *Miscellaneous printed materials.*   These include house organs—a publication about the company itself in the form of a brochure, newsletter, or magazine—or annual reports. Other types of printed material may also fall under this category.

- *Event marketing.*   Event marketing has become very popular. The idea is to have the marketer link the product to an event (e.g., the Olympics, Superbowl, World Series, College World Series of Advertising, and Students in Free Enterprise National Competition). Although any event can be used, the popularity of sporting events has made them more desirable. There tends to be more coverage and thus more reach for a particular message.

- *News pegs.*   Much like event marketing, a news peg attempts to create ties to a story that is very newsworthy. Many marketers have tied their news pegs into the event marketing activities discussed previously. Betty Crocker created an annual bake-off, giving a major prize to the winner. Other companies have created "hotlines" during events to generate additional reach for their message.

- *Posters.* Posters are a fairly popular way to communicate with the public (internally as well as externally). Many types of information can be placed on posters and then given, and in some instances sold, to consumers.
- *Exhibits.* Exhibits can help generate publicity for businesses. Binney & Smith of Easton, Pennsylvania, created a Crayola Factory in downtown Easton (the headquarters of the company). The factory was opened in conjunction with local economic development councils, and it shows the manufacturing process for a number of its products, especially Crayola crayons. The company then opened a retail store next door to the factory to facilitate sales and usage of their products. The factory has been a huge success. Hershey Foods, in Hershey, Pennsylvania, wanted to give consumers guided tours of the chocolate-making process, but their plants were too small to cover the demand. Also, Hershey wanted to maintain a maximum amount of security for their production processes. The tactic it used was to open a simulated factory, through which visitors ride. The ride ends at the factory store, where literally thousands of Hershey products can be purchased. Both of these public relations exhibits are extremely successful.
- *Miscellaneous audio visuals.* In addition to the electronic media kits, some organizations offer videotapes and films about the organization to the consumer. These are provided without cost (although some companies charge for postage) to individuals who have an interest in the organization. One of the larger customers for these types of audiovisual materials are colleges and universities.

As usual, the IMC public relations planner should include samples of the creative tactics involved in the overall process. A sample electronic press kit, news release, poster, and so on will help persuade the decision makers.

RATIONALE

Include a rationale for each of the tactical undertakings. If a common tactic is used in the industry but you don't want it, explain why. Any programs should have a budget and expected outcomes, both short-term and long-term. A flowchart of all consumer PR activities should be developed, including time lines and costs for each event. Tie-ins with other IMC areas should also be spelled out in the chart. The integration of all IMC areas has to be visual.

EVALUATION

There must be some degree of measurability for each of the PR tactics. The measurement is generally tied to the objectives given at the beginning of the plan. Short-term and long-term outcomes should be spelled out for the reader. How do they or will they know that the program has achieved its objectives?

Finally, there has to be integration throughout the entire PR process. A general overview of each of the activities could be included in the plan. Trade and consumer PR could be tied together by a flowchart, graph, or some other figure. Time lines should be indicated so that all areas of the IMC mix can be exploited to the company's advantage.

Figure 8–1 was created for a PR plan. Fill in the blanks. Don't forget to include flowcharts and graphs if they will help readers understanding the process. You, as the IMC manager, will also be able to utilize these flowcharts to help your overall management function.

FIGURE 8–1 Public Relations for the Trade and Final Consumer: A Template

Trade:

Objectives:

Strategies:

Tactics:

Rationale (Include Flowcharts, Graphs, Tables, etc.):

Evaluation Methods:

Consumer

  Objectives:

Strategy:

Tactical Executions (Provide Examples):

Rationale (Provide Documentation and/or Graphs, Flowcharts, Figures, etc.):

Evaluation Methods:

Integration of Trade and Consumer PR:

CHAPTER

Bringing It All Together 9

EVALUATION AND MEASUREMENT OF THE IMC PLAN

The final step in the IMC planning process (and any planning process, for that matter) is the development of evaluative techniques needed to identify the outcomes of the plan. The planner must evaluate the objectives, strategies, budget, and tactics of each of the variable areas to be sure that each program is obtaining the desired result. In general, the company should ask if it has achieved the overall goals set for the IMC function. Has the overall marketing plan been followed and the goals achieved? Was the IMC plan effective? If not, what outside influences may have had an impact on the IMC and marketing activities? Were they avoidable? How did the targeted markets and targeted audiences respond to the IMC activities? Additional general questions may be asked that assess the effectiveness of overall strategies. Although every program and plan should be evaluated for effectiveness, it is most crucial with a communications program. Communication measures are based on sales figures, as well as such nonsales figures as brand awareness; message comprehension; attitude changes toward the product, brand, company, or service; and purchase and intentions. If targeted levels are achieved, the evaluation program shows that the objectives were reached and the strategies and tactics were successful. Corrective action is required, however, for a plan that doesn't meet the stated objectives. Perhaps there needs to be a different combination of communication elements, revised strategies, or revised budgetary allocations.

This chapter describes some additional reasons for undertaking an evaluative program. In addition, methods for measurement are discussed in more detail, as well as auditing and testing methods.

EVALUATION

There are a number of very good reasons for providing measurement of the effectiveness of marketing programs. There are also some reasons for not doing so. The reasons for evaluation are as follows:

- ***Increasing the value and productivity of the IMC campaign.*** Because professionals involved in IMC are motivated, creative, and hard-working, there is a tendency for them to get wrapped up in a campaign. Sometimes they lose objectivity because of their closeness to the projects. An evaluation of the work can show these individuals if they're on the right track, or if they need to adjust some of their thoughts to achieve the overall goals of the clients.
- ***Avoiding mistakes.*** Mistakes in IMC can be costly. A great deal of money is expended on IMC activities each year (estimated to be close to $200 billion). The

need for evaluation becomes obvious as the managers strive to assure the clients that the money invested is being used in the most productive and cost-efficient manner. If mistakes in IMC executions can be avoided, there could be savings in the millions for any given company.

- *Increasing the effectiveness of strategies and tactics.* Evaluation can provide a tool for measuring which strategies and tactics will work best. In addition, the strategies and tactics can be tested after implementation to see if they were the most effective choices for the IMC planners.

Sometimes evaluation isn't used. Companies don't evaluate because of the following:

- *Cost.* Evaluative and research studies can be expensive. Unless directed to do so, many firms don't believe the investment is worth the benefit. Someone has to pay for the cost of the research, and this someone is often the client. By building the cost into the overall budget, some bids by certain IMC planners may be higher than those of the competition, thus, in theory, losing a client. Also, many IMC firms believe that the benefit is not worth the extra cost of evaluation. They feel that the time spent on evaluation could be better spent on campaign creation.

- *Objectivity.* Numerous creative people don't believe that the evaluation methods are accurate or objective. They feel that they are better able to judge their work than non-professionals.

- *Time.* Any evaluation takes time. Many judgments have to be made quickly, and the executives must be flexible in making decisions. Because of this time variable, many people do not undertake the necessary evaluative steps to ensure a productive campaign.

- *Reliability and validity.* Many IMC planners feel that the methodologies used in advertising and IMC testing are invalid and don't represent actual feelings or attitudes toward the campaigns.

- *What to test.* Simply put, many organizations don't know what to test.

Although these problems and issues may be inherent in many organizations, these are not good reasons for not evaluating the effectiveness of the IMC programs. Evaluating programs leads to more informed decision making, which in turn leads to increased productivity and profits for all involved. The research can help the integrated marketing communicators justify the return on the IMC campaign objectives. In addition, the information generated can be shared with other members of the management staff. Simply stated, one must evaluate one's programs in order to generate more effective and productive outcomes.

Objectives

To have an effective evaluation, you must develop objectives that are to be achieved in this process. As in all other areas of IMC, evaluation must also be evaluated. The easiest and most common method of evaluation is to compare the campaign results with the campaign objectives. If these weren't met, there is a problem that must be solved. Evaluation should occur at all levels of the campaign, so the researcher should set objectives for each level.

Methods

Many methods are used to evaluate campaign effectiveness. The next section will describe certain testing techniques that can be effective in assessing the IMC program. The timing of the evaluations is important. Testing should be an ongoing process in which the IMC communicators can tell how effective the program appears to be throughout (and after) the campaign. Before the executions, some type of concept testing should be involved. Are the concepts that were developed sound? Do they hold up under evaluation and testing? After the concept has been found to be sound, copy testing should be undertaken. Does the copy provide the right message to the audience? Does it convey the intended message? After media placement, the campaign can be tested by using some type of concurrent method. Finally, after the campaign, posttesting should be undertaken.

TESTING

There are many different types of tests for the research involved in developing and executing an IMC campaign. The methods must go through a series of steps, just as have the other elements of the campaign. Objectives must be set for the tests to be administered, and then a strategy must be developed. The actual testing is the execution or tactical variable. Certain types of tests work better with specific IMC functions. This section provides examples of tests that may be developed and used to help make the IMC campaign more effective.

Objectives and Strategies

Objectives for each of the areas to be tested are essential. The objectives should indicate what is to be achieved by the tests. They must be quantified, if possible, and measurable. In addition, they must be realistic. I suggest including an explanation of why the testing is being done, as well as a short explanation of the testing techniques to be used. The strategies should explain how the objectives will be met.

Methods

Methodologies for testing are also called testing tactics. In the methodology section, a flowchart should indicate when the tests will take place. Various testing methodologies are explained in the next few pages. The methods outlined are the more popular methods used in testing campaign effectiveness (as well as market testing). More techniques are available, and I encourage those interested to develop techniques of their own that will add credibility and productivity to IMC campaigns.

Concept Testing

In the initial phases of IMC plan development, managers are interested in the value of the concept they plan to use for the campaign. A good time to test for this concept is after market research and the situational analysis have been completed. Before expenditures on creative executions occur, the IMC manager can test the concept of the campaign—in other words, get a feel from the consumers about the campaign's concept. This process is called concept testing. The primary objective is to check on strategies, although this test can also be used for tactics. The following methods can meet this objective:

    Focus groups
    Mall intercepts
    In-depth interviews
    Scaling
    Questionnaires
    Rating scales
    Paired comparison
    Projective techniques

Remember that concept tests are developed with just a concept in mind. This concept is written down on a sheet of paper and then discussed or tested through selected members of the target audience. The test is qualitative and should give the researcher a feel for the consumers' attitudes. These tests can be completed fairly quickly with minimal investment.

Copy Testing

Copy testing is used to evaluate the impact of specific advertisements, such as thumbnail, rough, slick, or fully completed ads. The idea is to get feedback on the effectiveness of the specific ads before they're placed in the media. This type of testing is also known as pretesting. The following are some of the more common types of copy tests:

> Theater tests
> Central location tests
> Objective tests
> > Pupilometer (PSR), meaning pupil dilation response
> > Eye camera
> > T-scope (tachistoscope)
> > Galvanic skin response (GSR)
> Various television tests

Concurrent Tests

Concurrent tests are used while the advertising or IMC campaign is being run. The idea behind concurrent testing is that the advertising and other IMC executions can be modified or changed according to test results. There are two major methods of testing the IMC program while it's in progress: *coincidental studies* and *tracking studies.*

Coincidental Studies

Coincidental studies are used as a measurement tool while the consumers are being exposed to the various media utilized in the IMC campaign. The idea is to measure the amounts of exposure to the various executions and to measure reactions to the vehicles. The most common coincidental studies (and also the most effective) are used for broadcast advertising. The telephone study is the main method of coincidental study. Members of the targeted audience are called during airings of the advertisement. This allows the researcher to find out information as to what stations are being listened to or watched, and the IMC planner can determine whether or not the message is being heard or seen. A side benefit is that the researcher can reduce the amount of error associated with a subject's memory loss when tested at some later time period. The use of coincidental studies has declined in recent years, mostly because of the lack of additional information that can be obtained with this approach. The benefit may not be worth the cost.

Tracking Studies

Tracking studies are generally a series of interviews that are run with members of the targeted audience during the entire length of a campaign. Researchers can ascertain the effect of the campaign and the amount of exposure it is generating for the targeted audience. A predetermined schedule should always be followed for the studies to be effective. In particular, tracking studies provide the IMC planners with data about (1) product satisfaction (or dissatisfaction), (2) consumer awareness levels, (3) consumer attitudes, (4) consumer desires, (5) product usage, and (6) feedback. There are numerous methods of collecting these data; the most popular are the following:

- *Pantry checks.* Where the researcher physically goes to the targeted consumers' homes and records the brands of products they have, or the researcher simply asks what types of products and brands the consumers have.
- *Dust bin checks.* This is an alternative method of the pantry check. Consumers are asked to name packages of products that they have used over a predetermined period of time. Researchers physically pick up these packages and count the different types of brands and products to determine product usage.

- *Consumer diaries.* Consumers are told to keep a record of all activities involved in the purchase and use of certain brands of products (or product categories). The diary may include information on types of brands purchased, brand switching, coupons, and perhaps media usage.
- *Mall intercepts.* Although only occasionally used for tracking studies, mall intercepts are utilized to gain immediate information about the target audience.
- *Scanner data.* Companies such as Information Resources, Inc., and Nielsen Media Research generate data on product sales and movement by the use of a scanner. These data are then sold to IMC researchers who want to check the effectiveness of their IMC campaigns. As of this writing, Nielsen and Lucent Technologies are studying an agreement to develop the technologies and increased accuracy for additional scanning and media data.

Posttesting

Although it's much the same as concurrent testing, posttesting traditionally occurs after the campaign has ended. The basis for both posttesting and concurrent testing is to assess the impact of the campaign, after the audience has been exposed. Researchers assess the impact of the communications on the targeted audience and measure any behavioral changes that may have occurred as a result of the IMC campaign. To test behavior changes, researchers generally look at sales and product inquiries. To assess the communication effects, the areas of recognition and recall are studied as well as, to some extent, awareness and attitude.

The major drawback to posttesting is the lack of a base, or benchmark, from which to assess any changes. To avoid this potential problem, posttesting is conducted along with concurrent testing. Also, some researchers have begun to utilize the pre-posttest. With pre-posttesting, a sample is studied before the IMC campaign is launched, and the researcher can use it as a benchmark. Each of the IMC variables must be subject to the evaluation.

A number of companies exist for the sole purpose of providing information and data to individuals involved with IMC. These companies provide either *syndicated data* or *customized information.* The main companies involved in this area of information are:

Starch
Gallup & Robinson
Nielsen
Information Resources, Inc. (IRI)
ASI Market Research, Inc.
McCollum/Spielman
American Research Systems (ARS)
American Research Foundation (ARF)
Simmons Market Research Bureau (SMRB or Simmons)
Arbitron
Mediamark Research, Inc. (MRI)

This is a small sample of the companies interested in marketing communication research; there are many more. Appendix A lists additional sources that may be used in developing evaluation techniques for your plan. Many college and university professors are interested in doing research projects for companies in areas of their expertise and interest. Professors may be especially helpful when customized studies are required.

The IMC planners must recognize the importance and value of the testing and measurement of their campaigns. There must be some sort of assessment or evaluative tool in place to justify the tactics used in creating the campaign. A good system for evaluation and control should be built in to the overall campaign and integrated into all strategic plans. The evaluation and control systems will improve productivity and effectiveness for most IMC campaigns.

Figure 9–1 allows evaluation and testing. Fill in the blanks in order to have an effective and well-planned evaluation process.

LEGAL ISSUES

One final caveat should be made. As consumerism gains ground, there will be more and more legislation aimed at advertisers and IMC planners. You, as an IMC professional, should be aware of the potential impact legislation and consumerism could have on your profession. Certain pieces of legislation mandate research and evaluation. To protect yourself from potential lawsuits and threats, you should be familiar with some of the laws and government bodies that may have an impact on any IMC professional. Listed are various federal agencies, legislation, and issues that could possibly have a direct connection to your campaign. Be sure you are aware of these regulations or agencies, and study their impact on your IMC plan.

I recommend that you get a copy of the Federal Trade Commission (FTC) industry guides for your particular client:

- Postal Fraud Laws
- Copyright Act of 1976
- Restrictions on PUFFERY
- Federal Food, Drug, and Cosmetic Act
- Bait-and-Switch Advertising
- FTC Mail Order Rule
- Credit Advertising (Truth in Lending Act)
- Leasing (Under Truth in Lending Act Regulations M and Z)
- *Guides Concerning Use of Endorsements and Testimonials in Advertising* (part of the FTC)
- Food and Drug Administration
- Lanham Trademark Act
- Various Consumer Sales Practices Acts (adopted state by state)
- Uniform Deceptive Trade Practices Acts (adopted state by state)
- Various Statewide Consumer Fraud Acts
- Impact of Product Liability on Advertising
- Rights of Privacy
- Right of Publicity
- Federal Trademark Act of 1946
- Standards of Comparative Advertising
- Legal Ramifications of Contests and Lotteries (note the U.S. Postal Service; Federal Communications Commission; Bureau of Alcohol, Tobacco, and Firearms; and the Federal Trade Association—all have some regulatory power over contests and lotteries)
- The Impact of Guarantees and Warranties (in particular, Consumer Products Warranty Act of 1975 and Magnuson-Moss Warranty Act)
- The Magnuson-Moss Warranty Act
- Nondisclosure Agreements
- Client-Agency Law
- Breach of Contract
- Ads Directed at Children
- False, Misleading, or Deceptive Ads
- Codes of Ethics
- Alcohol and Tobacco Advertising

THE END . . . OR THE BEGINNING

You now have all the information necessary to develop and execute an effective and integrated marketing communications plan. I hope that you were filling in the templates as you went along. If not, take time in the upcoming days or weeks to fill in the blanks that you've omitted. Your plan will help guide you along your journey as an IMC professional. This road map will help you chart your course for today, tomorrow, and the future. Remember, when developing IMC plans, above all, have fun.

I'll end this book with a few hints and tips that may help you to create a better working IMC plan document. The plan is to be used by you, but it will need approval from many different sources. The more that is succinct, the more that gets read and approved.

DOC'S TIPS AND HINTS FOR WRITING THE INTEGRATED MARKETING COMMUNICATION PLAN

- Utilize the templates in this book as an outline before putting together a finished document.
- Realize that the IMC plan is dynamic. Things change. Adjust the plan as necessary while completing it. There may have to be last-minute (or last-second) changes, caused by changes in the marketing environment.
- Utilize as many tables, figures, and graphs as possible. Include as many flowcharts as possible to help the reader understand what you're trying to say. Flowcharts help give the reader a sense of the time necessary for campaign development.
- In all cases use the KISS principle (keep it simple, stupid). In other words, be brief.
- Keep your situational analysis concise and full of facts, not guesses.
- Avoid redundancy. Try not to repeat the same thing over and over.
- Do not use personal pronouns (e.g., "We have a plan"). Readers know who wrote the plan.
- Begin with the most important things. Use a rationale and research for all your points.
- Put an executive summary at the beginning of the plan.
- Use primary research as much as possible to support your claims.
- Keep your objectives to the point. If possible, keep them to one sentence or less.
- Show as many creative executions (tactics) as possible.
- Show all sources of information that are not common knowledge.
- Keep the plan to a 60-page maximum (the American Advertising Federation's National Student Advertising Competition–College World Series of Advertising, limits the number of pages—generally to 40).
- Be sure to recheck your media plan. It must deliver the reach, frequency, and GRPs that you've claimed in order to achieve the other IMC objectives.
- Include the measurement and evaluation tools that will be used throughout the campaign. Justify their use. Explain how you will control the campaign should problems occur, based on the measurement and evaluation tools.
- Provide a rationale for all objectives, strategies, and tactics.
- Be sure the entire campaign book is integrated. Point out how you're achieving synergy with the campaign.
- Point out your unique selling point. Be sure you close the pitch. Why should your plan be chosen over those of the competition?
- Be creative.
- Above all, be positive.

FIGURE 9–1 Evaluation and Testing in IMC Planning: A Template

Evaluation:

Objectives:

Methods:

Testing:

Objectives and Strategies:

Methodology:

APPENDIX

Methods and Sources for the Company Analysis

The best place to start securing data for the company analysis is a library. Some type of cumulative book index or print-based index is available at almost all libraries. Many libraries also offer an electronic data-search vehicle, accessed by a computer. These searches are generally available in two formats: online or CD-ROM. Some of the online vendors that are useful are Dialog, LEXIS/NEXIS, and the Dow Jones Retrieval Service. Use *Books in Print* to find out which books are available on a given subject. For specific journal or newspaper articles, the *Funk and Scott Index of Corporations and Industries* is useful, as are the *Business Periodical Index* and the *Wall Street Journal Index*. Finally, ask a reference librarian to assist you in your search for information. The data search should be categorized by the major types of information required for a thorough analysis. For example, company information and financial information could become two separate categories. The following outline and explanation should help in the search for data.

1. Financial information
   a. Moody's manuals. Moody's offers numerous volumes of financial and operating information for over 30,000 companies and 20,000 government bodies. Each manual is published annually; however, updates are available as often as every week.
      (1) *Moody's Industrial Manual*
      (2) *Moody's Transportation Manual*
      (3) *Moody's Public Utility Manual*
      (4) *Moody's OTC Industrial Manual*
      (5) *Moody's Bank and Financial Manual*
      (6) *Moody's Municipal and Government Manual*
      (7) *Moody's OTC Unlisted Manual*

   b. Standard and Poor's data. Standard and Poor's provides financial data on 11,000 publicly held companies. The entries are updated annually; however, a publication entitled *The Daily News Service* is published daily. In this publication, changes in corporation entries are kept up to date.
      (1) *Standard and Poor's Corporation Records*
      (2) *Standard and Poor's Over-the-Counter Regional Exchange Reports*
      (3) *Standard and Poor's American Stock Exchange Reports*
      (4) *Standard and Poor's New York Stock Exchange Reports*
   c. Disclosure database. Disclosure provides managerial and financial information on about 12,000 publicly held corporations. This database is available either online or as a CD-ROM.
   d. Valueline. The *Valueline Investment Survey* is available in print, online, and as a CD-ROM. Valueline provides in-depth reports on about 2,000 companies and corporations. The company summaries are updated quarterly.

2. Company-specific information
   a. Prospectuses
   b. Annual reports (in print or on the Internet)
   c. House organs
   d. Internet (Begin by accessing the government's *Internet Edgar Dissemination* project)
      (1) World Wide Web: http://www.town.hall.org/edgar/edgar.html
      (2) Gopher: gopher://town.hall.org
      (3) Anonymous ftp: ftp.town.hall.org
   e. National Trade Data Bank (can be accessed through the World Wide Web: http://www.stat-usa.gov/BEN/Services/ntdbhome.html)

APPENDIX

Research Methods for the Product Evaluator

1. Qualitative research techniques. Qualitative research, sometimes called exploratory research, is used to explore for ideas or insights into customers. It is not intended to be "hard" research. Samples are limited, and the research is mostly objective. The following are common techniques for generating qualitative research.

   a. One-on-one (or in-depth) interview. This interview is run by a trained professional, who asks a consumer various unstructured questions to gain insights into consumers' attitudes, problems, motives for buying, and so on. Probing by the interviewer is required.

   b. Focus groups. This research is also an in-depth interview, but with many individuals (usually 7–11). The group members have to be representative of the consumer population. The meeting generally lasts from one to three hours. There should be an outline of what information is needed. From that outline a trained moderator begins the discussion, but then is careful not to join in the conversation. The moderator should only steer the group in the right direction.

   c. Ethnography. Ethnography is the description and classification of ethnic groups, specifically, races and cultures. In ethnography, researchers try to get as close as possible to current or potential users of a product or service. The researcher goes to the consumer's environment for an in-depth look at the consumer's decision-making process. Ethnography involves observation and questioning. The researcher also takes numerous photographs to study.

   d. Projective tests
      (1) Sentence completion
      (2) Story completion
      (3) Word association

2. Quantitative research techniques

   a. Survey research
      (1) Telephone interviews
      (2) Mail questionnaires
      (3) Personal interviews (primarily mall intercept studies)
      (4) Internet questionnaires

   b. Scaling techniques for survey responses
      (1) Semantic differential scales. These are scales that list a series of bipolar responses (usually adjectives or phrases) that are separated by some given rating scale (usually 7 or 9 points). The scale is used to measure the consumer's attitude toward a product, company, or service.

      Example: My university is

      Friendly _ _ _ _ _ _ Unfriendly
      Beautiful _ _ _ _ _ _ Ugly
      Exciting _ _ _ _ _ _ Boring

      (2) Stapel scales. These scales measure the respondents' agreement or disagreement with a product, product idea, service, phrase, or word.

      (3) Likert-type scales. The respondent is asked to indicate levels of agreement or disagreement about many statements. Usually the responses are limited to "strongly agree," "agree," "neutral," "disagree," and "strongly disagree."

APPENDIX

Sources for Consumer Analysis

Although there are additional sources, the following are those usually used to generate consumer data.

1. Demographic data
   a. Simmons Market Research Bureau (SMRB), *Study of Media and Markets*
   b. Mediamark Research, Inc. (MRI)
   c. U.S. Bureau of the Census
2. Psychographic data
   a. Simmons
   b. VALS 2. This is actually a system designed and developed by SRI International to help segment markets based on psychographics.
   c. Standard Rate and Data Service (SRDS), Lifestyle Market Analysis
   d. The Sourcebook of ZIP Code Demographics (put out by CACI Marketing Systems)

3. Geodemographics
   a. Claritas's PRIZM (Potential Rating Index by Zip Markets). This research group has broken down the over 500,000 U.S. neighborhoods into 40 basic clusters. Each of these clusters has been given a very descriptive name.
   b. Donnelly Marketing Information Services' ClusterPLUS. Provides the same type of information as PRIZM.
   c. Geo Vals. This method was developed by SRI International and Market Statistics. The system estimates the numbers and percentages of VALS segments in geographic regions throughout the United States. These data can be accessed through mapping or spreadsheet software.

APPENDIX

Media Terms and Definitions

The following list provides terms and definitions often used in the development of media schedules, objectives, and plans. This list is not inclusive, but it does contain the most utilized terms.

Area of dominant influence (ADI): Arbitron-developed, mutually exclusive, geographic communication area. *All* counties in the United States are assigned to an ADI, depending on their main source of media communication.

Audience: Homes, or individuals watching, reading, seeing, or listening to a given media vehicle.

Audience composition: Audience demographics.

CATV: Community Antenna Television Service. See Cable television.

Cable television (Cable TV): A broadcasting system that distributes channels to individual homes through coaxial cable. The cable companies often receive signals, which they distribute, from satellites. The programs that are distributed are gathered by a community antenna (CATV).

Cost-per-rating-point (C/RP): The overall cost of buying one percentage point of a TV home (or individual viewer). The cost is for a given time period and for a given program type.

Coverage: Audience reach in numbers.

Cumulative audience (CUME): Essentially the same as reach. This is the net unduplicated audience of a campaign (either in one medium or a combination of media). The cume audience is also referred to as an unduplicated or net audience.

Designated market area (DMA): As with an ADI, a mutually exclusive, geographic market area, for television, as defined by Nielsen. Counties are assigned a DMA according to their total viewing hour percentages. Media can be purchased according to their DMAs. For example, a media buyer may want to purchase the top 100 DMAs.

Effective frequency: The total number of exposures needed to elicit change in the targeted audience (or market).

Effective reach: The percentage of the target audience that has been exposed to an advertising schedule enough times to elicit some type of change in behavior (e.g., awareness, attitude, or purchase decision).

Exclusivity: A major monetary commitment to purchase space or time to allow an advertisement to be free of competing advertising.

First-run syndication: Shows that are produced specifically for the syndication market (see Syndication). These are original shows.

Frequency distribution: The number of homes (or individuals) exposed to a given media schedule, arranged by the number of times exposed.

Gross impressions: The same as gross audience. The total number of all audiences exposed to all media vehicles in a given media plan.

Households (or homes) using television (HUT): The total percentage of homes using TV sets at a given time.

Impressions: The total number of exposures given for a particular medium.

Index: A system developed to provide the advertiser and marketer with information about something, tied to a base number. In an index, the base number is generally 100, which provides an average. Anything over 100 (101 and up) is above average, and anything below 100 (99 or less) is below average. The numbers indicate how close to average the item under study is. For example, for a particular market, the index number for women aged 18–25 is 120. This indicates that, all else being equal, this could be an outstanding market for products being targeted to this age group.

LNA–BAR (Leading National Advertiser–Broadcaster Reports): A research source that provides, for a fee, information and analysis for television and network radio. This is a good source of competitive spending.

Network: A group of stations (two or more) under contract, or ownership, that broadcast programs. The major networks are ABC, CBS, and NBC, although Fox and UPN are becoming more popular. There are also a number of smaller networks that have been developed within the past few years (CNBC, CNN, BET, A&E, TNN, TNT, USA, and the Weather Channel, to name only a few).

Network affiliate: A station that is part of the overall network and thus offers network programs.

Outdoor advertising: Advertising that is placed outdoors (billboards, posters, signs, paintings on barns, etc.).

Outdoor plant: A company specializing in the sale or maintenance (including construction) of outdoor displays (mostly dealing with painted displays or posters).

Out-of-home audience: Audiences that are exposed to publications and radio (including battery-operated or in the car) outside of their own homes.

Radio dayparts: The different times of day identified for more accurate media planning and scheduling. Radio dayparts are M–F 6 A.M. to 10 A.M.—morning drive time; M–F 10 A.M. to 3 P.M.—midday; M–F 3 P.M. to 7 P.M.—afternoon drive time; M–Sunday 7 P.M. to midnight—evening; Saturday and Sunday 6 A.M. to 7 P.M.—weekend.

Rating: The percentage of a given population that has been exposed to a broadcast or single-print publication issue.

Rating/HUT/share: The formula given as Rating = HUT × share.

Reach: The number of different individuals (or in some cases, homes) that were exposed to an advertising message (or schedule) at least one time. Reach is almost always expressed as a percentage of the population.

Run of schedule (ROS): A broadcast commercial without a specified time slot or period. The station may run the advertisement whenever it feels it is appropriate. The time period may very from day to day or week to week. For the media planner, this is the most cost-efficient way to purchase spot radio and television.

Sets in use: The total number of television sets tuned in to a given program during a given time of day (and/or day of week). This term used to be synonymous with HUT, but because of the numbers of households watching different programs, sets in use deals only with TV sets, not households.

Showing: The number of cards in transit advertising included in the overall unit of sale or the number of posters (in outdoor advertising) sold as a unit.

Spot (television and radio): Various broadcast station times bought market by market.

Syndication: The purchase or sale of programs on a market-by-market basis. The syndicated market includes over 200 TV markets.

Television dayparts: Generally, the units of a broadcast day. For television the dayparts are generally daytime (which includes the morning and afternoon), early fringe time, prime time, and late fringe time.

Zapping: Television commercial audiences who switch channels (generally by remote control, although it could be done manually) to avoid commercials. Zapping also occurs when audiences record a program (i.e., by VCR) and delete the commercials.

Zipping: Zipping occurs when the audience avoids the commercials or advertisements on recorded programs (i.e., on the audience's VCRs or other devices). The audience "zips" by the commercial, utilizing the fast-forward function on the VCR or remote control.

APPENDIX

Advantages and Disadvantages of Select Media

MAGAZINES

Advantages

Special interests and demographic audiences can be targeted. Copy can be tailored to these groups.

Ads can be of high quality and very appealing to audiences.

New technologies allow more attention-getting advertisements (pop-ups, sampling, fold-outs, etc.).

Magazines are good for prestige products.

Magazines are good for image development IMC campaigns.

There is good geographic selectivity for city magazines.

Magazines allow long shelflife, and thus long ad life.

Magazines allow extended, in-depth copy.

Disadvantages

There has been a trend toward increased CPMs.

Magazines may miss a lot of their targeted audience. (e.g., *Esquire* reaches only about 2 percent of adult males).

Prices are increasing.

Frequency is limited.

There is a lot of clutter.

Readership is low. According to research only about 3 percent of media time is spent in reading magazines.

Copy must be prepared well in advance of publication.

NEWSPAPERS

The newspaper is a traditional medium, with wide acceptance and credibility.

Newspapers have good reach.

Newspapers are good for detailed communication messages.

There is excellent flexibility: Ads can be changed easily.

Newspapers provide a good vehicle for couponing.

There is good visual impact. Some color is available.

The size of the advertisement can be tailored.

Some demographic targeting can be based on different sections of the paper.

There is clutter, as well as no competitive protection.

Coupon redemption rates are declining.

Circulations are not keeping pace with population growth.

Rates are increasing.

The numbers of dailies are being reduced.

Many young adults do not read the paper.

Readers don't read the entire paper.

Newspapers are a passive medium. It is hard to create buyer action or demand.

OUTDOOR

Advantages

Ads are low cost, based on CPM.

Ads have excellent impact because of size.

Specific geographic areas can be targeted (e.g., neighborhoods or entire cities).

Ads are attention grabbing.

Simple ads are very effective.

Ads can include additional attention getters (e.g., temperature or time).

Disadvantages

Ads must be brief.

Ads are inflexible.

Effectiveness is related to traffic flows and weather.

Venue may have a negative image in some markets.

There is low recall.

There is limited availability.

YELLOW PAGES

This provides very effective reach for those consumers who are ready to make a purchase.

Detailed information is possible.

Upper-income adults are users.

There is high penetration of the market.

This medium is useful for sought-after goods and services such as doctors, lawyers, plumbers, and pizza.

Good geographical selectivity is possible.

This is a passive medium.

It is hard to measure results.

Ads are mostly limited to home and work

There is too much clutter; ads are next to those of competitors.

There is low consumer influence.

The medium is inflexible.

TELEVISION

Broadcast

This is a show-and-tell medium.

It is used by more people than any other medium (approximately 4.2 hours per day).

It has excellent reach.

It has high impact.

A good product or service image can be created.

Many different selling messages can be created, including a complete selling story.

The CPM is high.

Flexibility is low.

There is increasing use of zipping and zapping.

There is clutter.

Recall is somewhat low.

Production costs are high.

There is seasonal viewing.

It doesn't reach upper-income adults effectively.

Cable

There is an increasing audience; there are over 60 million cable subscribers.

Penetration is high for the higher-income households.

There are fewer restrictions on creativity than in broadcast television.

The average cable household income is higher than noncable households (by almost 45 percent).

Ad rates are relatively low for the amount of reach.

There is a great deal of availability.

There may be inferior production quality.

There is more clutter than broadcast.

Rates are increasing.

It competes with broadcast television.

Pay channels are watched 33 percent of the time, thus reducing the number of those watching the ads.

RADIO

Advantages

Reach and frequency are good.

There is good demographic and geographic selectivity.

There is a low cost-per-thousand.

There is excellent flexibility: Messages may be changed at the last minute by the advertiser.

There is good local relevance.

If done properly, it can be a creative medium.

Disadvantages

There is too much clutter.

Commercials are short-lived.

It is a passive medium: Most listeners are doing other things when the radio is on.

It can have creativity restrictions.

Audiences are segmented. The advertiser may have to purchase many stations to reach the desired audience.

APPENDIX

Cyberspace Terminology

Address: The Internet site can be a set of numbers or someone's personal address, like `ogden@kutztown.edu`. When you see "com" at the end of an address, it usually represents a commercial site. "edu" indicates an educational institution, "gov" a government body, and "net" a network service provider.

Browser: This is the software used to navigate the databases. It gives the user a view into the databases through a series of rules for communication called protocols. The major protocols are: FTP, Telnet, Gopher, News-Network News Transfer Protocol (NNTP), and HTTP (Hypertext Transfer Protocol).

Client: A client is a computer that has access to cyberspace through a computer network's "server." Thus when you dial up a database, your system is the client and the system providing the information or data is the server (or host).

DNS (Domain Name System): This is the database of Internet names and addressees that translates names to official protocol numbers.

Home page: This is a company or organization's primary page of information about itself. It could be likened to a table of contents.

Hypertext: This is the system that provides electronic links from one online document to another.

The Internet: Also known as the Net, this is the global system, or collection, of computer networks that exchanges information through a protocol. The Internet consists of many internet-related networks called internets (with a lowercase *i,* as opposed to the Internet, with an upper-case I). Note that some internets are not connected to the Internet.

Internet access provider: This organization gives customers the ability to use one or more internet communication services such as E-mail, Gopher, and the Web.

Internet consultant: This organization helps clients obtain Internet access.

Servers: These are computer systems that manage and deliver information for client computers that are accessing the systems.

URL (Uniform Resource Locator): The address refers to a document or resource that is available through the Web (or the Internet). A URL contains information about the method of access, the server that must be accessed, and the path of the directories (or files) that are to be accessed on the server. The following list shows the type of organization a computer host is assigned:

Domain Name	Type of Host
com	commercial organization
edu	educational institution
gov	government agency
mil	U.S. military organization
net	network access providers
org	nonprofit organizations

Web: The Web is also known as the World Wide Web, WWW, or W3. It refers to all of the documents that are available on servers worldwide. Even more broadly, the Web can refer to all documents accessible through a Web browser. A single Web server may be called a web (notice the lowercase w, as opposed to the uppercase W for the World Wide Web).